Parent trek

D1300699

Parent trek

Nurturing creativity and care in our children

Jeanne Zimmerly Jantzi
Commissioned by Mennonite Central Committee

Herald
Press

Scottdale, Pennsylvania
Waterloo, Ontario

Library of Congress Cataloging-in-Publication Data

Jantzi, Jeanne Zimmerly, 1964-
    Parent trek: nurturing creativity and care in our children / Jeanne Zimmerly Jantzi.
      p. cm.
    Includes bibliographical references.
    ISBN 0-8361-9193-5 (alk. paper)
    1. Parenting—Religious aspects—Christianity. I. Title.
BV4529 .J36 2001
248.8'45—dc21   2001039548

The paper used in this publication is recycled and meets the minimum requirements of American National Standard for Information Sciences—Permanence of Paper for Printed Library Materials, ANSI Z39.48-1984.

Scripture marked (NRSV) is from the *New Revised Standard Version Bible*, copyright 1989 by the Division of Christian Education of the National Council of the Churches of Christ in the USA, and is used by permission, with all rights reserved. Scripture quotations marked (NIV) are from *The Holy Bible, New International Version*. Copyright © 1973, 1978, 1984 International Bible Society. Used by permission of Zondervan Bible Publishers. Verses marked (Living Bible) are taken from *The Living Bible* ©1971 owned by assignment by Illinois Regional Bank N.A. (as trustee). Used by permission of Tyndale House Publishers, Inc., Wheaton, IL 60189. All rights reserved.

No part of this publication may be reproduced, stored in a retrieval system, or transmitted in any form or by any means, electronic, mechanical, photocopying, recording, or otherwise, without the prior permission of the publisher or a license permitting restricted copying. Such licenses are issued on behalf of Herald Press by Copyright Clearance Center, Inc., 222 Rosewood Drive, Danvers, MA 01923; phone 978-750-8400; fax 978-750-4470; www.copyright.com.

PARENT TREK
Copyright © 2001 by Herald Press, Scottdale, Pa. 15683
    Published simultaneously in Canada by Herald Press,
    Waterloo, Ont. N2L 6H7. All rights reserved
Library of Congress Catalog Card Number: 2001039548
International Standard Book Number: 0-8361-9193-5
Printed in the United States of America
Book and cover design by Julie Kauffman

10 09 08 07 06 05 04 03 02 01   10 9 8 7 6 5 4 3 2 1

To order or request information, call 1-800-759-4447 (individuals); 1-800-245-7894 (trade). Website: www.mph.org

To Dan for your encouragement;
to Benjamin, David, and Paul for your energy and questions;
and to Glenn and Martha Zimmerly for your life example.

PREFACE

O ur children must create a new and different path if they are to live out the vision of enough for everyone. Our culture often encourages children to see themselves as consumers, to value individualism above community, and to believe that more is always better. If children are to challenge the status quo, they need a clear idea of how their lives fit with what they believe. They need self-confidence and the assurance that they can have an impact on the world.

The authors and contributors set out to provide a resource for adults interested in helping children develop the capacity to live creative, generous, joyful lives in a world of limits and great disparities. These capacities include:

valuing themselves,

connecting with others,

caring for creation,

thinking critically,

being creative.

The material in this resource comes from many voices. Mennonite Central Committee (MCC) asked for people's stories and experiences through Mennonite periodicals and the MCC alumni newsletter. Focus groups in the United States and Canada shared their thoughts with us. Authors wrote devotionals reflecting their experiences in light of Scripture.

The chapters follow the rhythms of life with children. Each chapter begins with a different author's short meditation to focus our thoughts. The discussion continues with a closer look at the topic and reflection questions woven throughout. Each chapter concludes with a collection of shared thoughts and experiences followed by a set of practical ideas to try. For further reading and investigation, check the resources for parents and children listed in the back.

This book invites you to take part in a conversation. It does not offer definitive answers to difficult questions. Instead, questions are posed and opinions shared for your journey. As contributor Susan Mark Landis wrote:

I am not so far along the road of living responsibly (no one with children calls it "simple!") as I would like to be, but the steps I take in the right direction are those I take with joy. It is when I look at options and say, "This one promotes a fuller life" that I know I won't be stepping backward from that decision after a few tries.

—*Jeanne Zimmerly Jantzi, author*

1.

sharing faith

Walk with children on the path of joyful obedience to God.

You shall put these words of mine in your heart and soul,
and you shall bind them as a sign on your hand, and fix them as an emblem on your forehead.
Teach them to your children, talking about them when you are at home
and when you are away,
when you lie down
and when you rise.
—Deuteronomy
11:18-19, NRSV

MEDITATION **the link to an enchanted world**

I asked our six-year-old son last night where and from whom he learns about God. He quickly listed the Bible, church people, and Sunday school teachers, in that order. I prompted a little: Do his parents ever talk about God? "Oh, yeah," he grinned, "and you're doing it right now!"

I like to talk about God with my two children. It's one way I share faith with them. Perhaps, like my own father, I am being faithful to God's instruction to Israel to teach its children about the commands and great deeds of the Lord "when you are at home and when you are away, when you lie down and when you rise." Perhaps. But maybe it is also because when we talk about God, my children share their faith with me.

My world is one of materials: building materials, issues of substance. When I talk to my children about God in my sparse, careful phrases, they talk back from a lush jungle of mysteries and wonder—where the impossible just is. At bedtime they have been known to divvy up the Trinity so that each has a comforter for the night—with one left over for Mom and Dad to share. Heaven, they inform me with certainty, contains cats that never bite. When they speak of their faith, a tropical breeze blows across my prairie winter. What, then, do I have to offer my children in return for their gift? Stories. If they have the wonder, I have the words. Not words to tame their visions, but words that help locate their experience of God in a larger story. Deuteronomy demands it. Stories of enslavement and liberation. Stories of idolatry and faithfulness. Stories of people who have fearlessly brought a child's faith with them into adulthood.

At age four my daughter decided to stop praying out loud. I worried briefly that she had rejected the piety that I was so carefully offering her. I wondered if I should insist. Now I have come to understand that she has a vital prayer life and always did. It's just that my listening was not essential to it. I want to introduce my daughter to the story of Hildegard of Bingen, a twelfth-century woman recognized to be so intimately conversant with God that her visions were broadcast across Europe. A woman who—like my daughter, who wants to be an author and illustrator—expressed her love for God by illuminating manuscripts.

In the same way I want to tell my son about his grandparents. Grandparents who participated in a war for which there was no justification. Grandparents who, many years later, courageously offered sanctuary to draft dodgers as an expression of their faith in the God of peace. I want to help my son see that he is not the first to live in the tension between what is and what ought to be; between the excitement he feels watching Luke Skywalker in battle and his oft-expressed hope that "there should never be another war."

The term *sharing* sometimes refers to a gift from one who has to one who has not. When we share faith with children, we each offer the other some of what we have. My children offer me a link to an enchanted world. I offer them stories in which they can root their experience and explore new possibilities.

—*Rick Zerbe Cornelsen*

With children, faith and values are more often caught than taught. This sets a high standard for parents, whose lives are under almost round-the-clock scrutiny by their children. If children are to live creative, generous lives, they need to be surrounded by adults who model creative, generous living. As our children imitate our values, what do they mirror back to us? Do our lives consistently show what we value?

The commercial world encourages values of consumption and finding fulfillment through possessions. Children often learn social roles, identity, values, and beliefs through the story lines of advertisements, TV, music, and movies.

In contrast, the needs and desires of people of faith are filled through Jesus. We want to root our stories in God's world. Often an action or an object provokes a child's question. One of our responses can be a faith story. In the book of Joshua, God instructs the people to take twelve stones from the middle of the Jordan so "When your children ask in time to come, 'What do those stones mean to you?' then you shall tell them . . ." (Josh. 4:6, NRSV). The children would notice the rock pile and be curious enough to ask, "Why?" Then the faith storytelling begins.

At our house, my three sons ask, "Why?" all the time. "Why are we eating leftovers?" "Why do you want me to take the late bus instead of coming to pick me up at school?" "Why are we going to visit the new family when we can't even speak their language?" There are faith reasons for all these actions. Yet too often, I brush off the questions. It takes a lot of mental energy to articulate the ways in which my faith connects with what I am doing.

Is there a faith reason for how many hours we work each week? For how we

how have you helped children see connections between faith and lifestyle?

spend our money? For the number of cars we own? For how we use energy? For how we measure success? For how many activities our children participate in? Do our children believe these decisions are simply family quirks or do they realize that they are faith-based decisions? As we live together from birth through the teen years, our children will catch on to *how* we do things in our family. Telling stories allows us to share with them *why* we do things.

What do we believe in? When do we say "Yes"? Faithful living is not focused on doing without, what we avoid, what we do not do, or what we shun. A faithful, abundant life is not spartan, austere, or insufficient. An abundant life says "Yes!" "Therefore do not worry, saying, 'What will we eat?' or 'What will we drink?' or 'What will we wear?' For it is the Gentiles who strive for all these things; and indeed your heavenly Father knows that you need all these things. But strive first for the kingdom of God and his righteousness, and all these things will be given to you as well" (Matt. 6:31-33, NRSV). We set our hearts on God's kingdom.

"The clear witness of Scripture is that something beyond good intentions and willpower is needed to transform our ego-centric, greed-captivated personalities into an all-inclusive community of loving, sharing persons."[1] Through sharing our faith in words and actions, we can point children toward God.

Our choice for movement toward God's kingdom is illustrated by a simple line drawing in the Good News version of the Bible. Deuteronomy 30:19 shows a figure dancing exuberantly, face uplifted and arms stretched open to the heavens. "I am now giving you the choice between life and death, between God's blessing and God's curse, and I call heaven and earth to witness the choice you make. Choose life!"

in your own life, what connections do you see between faith and simplicity?

what parts of your faith do you think can be caught by children in your family or church?

what parts of your faith do you explicitly teach them?

what faith stories do you want to pass on to children?

in what ways have children shared their faith with you?

passing thoughts

I am careful to explain to our daughter the **choices** I make—it's not because I'm cheap. It's that I'm choosing to try to live simply (1) so that we'll have more money to **share** with those in need, and (2) because I care about the environment. I try not to force my values upon my daughter, but rather to model what I feel is the best Christian approach to these issues.

—*Amarette Cummings*

We talk with our children about situations that come up with their friends, on the bus, at school, and at church. We have **role played** different ways of responding to teasing and a bully to help build confidence and a stronger voice.

We have endless discussions about race issues, words, and language they hear and the **w h y s** of everything they see. We admit that some things just don't have easy answers and we as parents don't always know answers.

—*Carol Martin Johnson*

Connecting our faith to lifestyle choices is not always easy to explain to children. They are much more conscious of what other families have and do than they are of faith concepts. Perhaps the best role **m o d e l** one can place before them is Jesus himself. The Gospel stories tell us clearly that he lived simply and frugally, not even owning a home.

—*Anette Eisenbeis*

Our eight-year-old began to complain about going to Sunday school and church. "I hate it. It's boring." What I knew intellectually suddenly became like a fist in the gut. Our children might make spiritual and lifestyle choices that are quite **d i f f e r e n t** from ours, and these are not on hold until they are adults! Little by little, as they become more and more independent, they make their own way. We can share with them the **j o y** we find in our choices, but then must step back and allow them to make their own.

—*Carol Loeppky*

Making choices for simple living is an ongoing process. How can we encourage our children to consider this process when we ourselves are being pulled in different directions every day? We hope we can convey our **i n t e n t i o n s**, if not solutions, to live reflecting our faith and hope to live in solidarity with our environment and community.

—*Brenda MacDonald*

We freely discuss social **j u s t i c e** issues of all sorts with our children. This usually arises when they ask some sort of question about something, like, "Where are my runners made?" Or "Why do we give our clothes to the women's shelter?" Or "Why do we give money to church?" We try to avoid being doctrinaire about it, but encourage **q u e s t i o n s** and discussions and different perspectives. *—Michelle Bull*

We try to emphasize the **j o y** and freedom that come with simple living as contrasted with the striving, accumulating ways of the culture around us. Our family slogan is: "**p e o p l e** before things." *—Andrea Gerber*

Kids love a sense of **b e l o n g i n g** . At this preschool stage, at least, it works to say, "Some families do it this way, but our family does . . ." It makes our young children feel as if they have a special place. *—Andrea Schrock Wenger*

I don't know what our children retained from what we said. What stuck is what they **s a w** and felt. We lived simply. We lived in a modest house and drove modest cars. Gladys was a very **r e s o u r c e f u l** homemaker. The boys helped with home repair, skills they practice to this day. *—Edgar Stoesz*

bring in the big picture. Use children's questions or comments as a springboard to talk about poverty, suffering, and ethical issues in the world you want them to learn about.

encourage children to share their faith. Ask them what they believe and why. Encourage them to tell others when their faith gives them a different point of view.

make it a special family thing. Some families do it this way, but our family does it another way because . . .

hear others' faith stories. Ask church members, grandparents, and extended family to share with children stories from their lives and experience.

encourage participation. Involve children in actions growing out of faith and simple living choices: household tasks, recycling, sharing with others, and learning home skills.

try this

answer "why?" with a story. Give children reasons for your beliefs and choices by telling stories of Jesus, of your family history, and of Christians today or long ago whose faith illuminated their choices.

role play situations with children. Give them ideas for responses to teasing or bullying, to racist comments or other put-downs, and to difficult situations they encounter at school or elsewhere.

2.

building self-esteem

Help children recognize that their worth comes from being children of Creator God.

Do not think of yourselves more highly than you ought,
but rather think of yourself with sober judgment,
in accordance with the measure of faith God has given you.
—*Romans 12:3b, NIV*

MEDITATION **frost patterns on the window**

"how I wish I'd listened to my children's feelings, and
let them have some input!" a Quaker woman said to
me when my children were young. This mother valued
simple living, taught her children, and lived her values.
Both her daughters, though, grew up to live lives of
conspicuous consumption. Her daughters had been
embarrassed to bring their friends over to a house with a
second-hand couch they hated. They resented doing without the things they craved. She wished she had listened to
these feelings and had let them take part in decisions.

This story has a major impact on my parenting. It is
not enough, I realize, to live my values; to prize faith and
generosity over things. Since my children will choose their
own values, simply imposing mine on them could backfire.
How can I help my children embrace Christlike values?

Jesus and Paul taught people to base their self-esteem on being children of God and having faith; not on ancestry, good works, or possessions. Our culture bombards us with other "necessities" to feel good: power, a sleek body, and the latest brand name. How can I help my children celebrate their God-given value and not seek other gods?

A poster in our laundry room reminds us that "It is not how much we have, but how much we enjoy, that makes happiness." We teach this in word, and let our children see us practice it. We show pleasure at frost patterns on the windows, at solving problems creatively within our value system, and in giving and receiving hugs—an important part of every day. We talk about happiness: half a cookie can be enjoyed thoroughly, while someone absorbed in other thoughts may wolf down several cookies without half the pleasure.

The Quaker woman might have done these things, but still her children rejected biblical values and clung to the world's values. In retrospect, she thought that if she had asked her children's feelings and had them participate in family decisions, they might have based their self-esteem on God's love rather than on flashy possessions. But how can I listen without judging? How can I accommodate the desires of my children while holding my values? How can I avoid forcing my values on them, yet share my values and live them freely?

I hope and pray that someday my children will have learned, as did Paul, "the secret of being content in any and every situation, whether well fed or hungry, whether living in plenty or in want," and that their confidence will come from knowing "I can do everything through him who gives me strength" (Phil. 4:12b-13, NIV).

—*Sue Klassen*

We want to help children learn to value themselves and to recognize that their worth comes from being children of God, the Creator. In a world where a person's worth is often defined by possessions, we hope children will develop a different frame of reference.

Children need the sustained support of their family and faith community in order to go against the mainstream of consumer culture. Going against the mainstream does not imply a constant battle of saying "no" all the time. Instead, it means helping children to think through who they are, what they believe, and what they are capable of doing. Building self-esteem begins in families when children are young and continues through supportive communities as they grow.

Families can be the springboard to launch children to confidently experience new things. The degree to which a child or adult takes risks and develops trust in self and others depends in large part on the environment that holds and supports each member.[1] Contributor Carol Martin Johnson wrote about helping her children develop skills in their urban setting:

We want our children to learn how to live in a scary world and not be paralyzed by fear. We teach them how to cross a street safely: to wait for the green light but not blindly trust it and to anticipate crazy drivers. We teach them to be cautious and smart and, in the end, confident. We teach them to be wary of strangers, but willing to greet people. We teach them everyday skills, and how to do them well. We teach our children to answer the phone confidently, to make phone calls, how to use a pay phone, and how to call home from a friend's house. We teach them to answer the front door, using a footstool when necessary to see

how have I included children in family decisions?

what are the voices that shape the values of the children close to me?

who is there before letting anyone in, and to memorize and write down the license plate of a dangerous driver.

Perhaps most importantly we are reminding them to trust their intuition: to tune in to and trust that voice inside and follow it, in spite of what voices and pressures on the outside are telling them.

Parents reaffirm their children's value by helping them gain competence in new skills, comforting them in times of disappointment, spending time with them, and listening carefully to them. Contributor Sue Klassen describes this as listening deeply.

When I listen, I try to reflect what I hear my child saying through words and body language. Sometimes what I hear changes my mind. My children feel good about themselves when I use an idea they had and find it works better than my way. My children need me to listen to their thoughts, feelings, and stories; to share who they are and who they are becoming. Frequently, I can listen superficially while doing other chores, but I find it important to snuggle up at bedtimes and some other times to listen with a full ear and heart.

At times, my children want something very badly or are hurting. Like any parent, I like to help fix the problem. But sometimes I am unable or unwilling to grant what they wish. Then, listening deeply is especially powerful. If a child wants a toy that goes against our values or a pet we cannot own, the issue can become all consuming. I know I need to take time for deep listening when I hear the same "tape" over and over, and my child follows me around to make sure I hear it. Then, I turn off the stove, let go of agenda, sit down beside my child, and say something like, "I see you really want such-and-so." "Yes," my child says, and

what options and ideas can help children think about how culture shapes their values?

then launches into a long, tearful explanation of why this is more important than anything.

I try to keep reflecting what I am hearing and avoid reasoning as much as possible. I occasionally say, "You know we will not do that because . . ." and list the reasons we have already been through many times. "But you still really want this?" This process usually takes ten minutes to half an hour, but the investment is well worth the time and tears. A healing takes place when someone feels heard at a deep level, and the issue loses its power. We can move beyond the stuck place, even though the wish is not granted or the problem is not fixed. My children walk with a taller bearing and look as if a great load has been lifted after such a time of listening. Being heard is an important building block of self-esteem.

Circles of relationships give children a sense of identity and belonging. As members of a loving community children can define who they are. One of my favorite hymns ends with this line: "There would I find a settled rest, while others go and come. No more a stranger, nor a guest, but like a child at home."[2] Carol Martin Johnson explains:

We rely heavily on our faith community where our children have friends of all ages, adults who love and care about them and talk to them. And where we have like-minded friends to process faith and lifestyle issues with those who are also striving to raise creative and loving children in our urban environment.

Carol Loeppky also wrote about the need to be part of a supportive community:

It is difficult not to get lured into the values of the world when you feel like the lone voice in the wilderness. It is especially difficult for a child or a teenager.

how can we help children think critically about where God's values and culture's values are opposed or in harmony?

Joyful living is easier and more joyful when shared. We don't isolate ourselves from others with different values, but we do try to spend more time with those who share our perspectives.

We want our children to be able to stand strong as God's own handiwork—not molded by a consumer or individualistic culture, but transformed by an inner sense of what is right.

sometimes people who value simple living derive self-worth from what they do not own, priding themselves that they are so unworldly. How can we avoid a fixation on things, either having them or not having them?

in my own childhood, how did my parents, church, community, and those significant in my life help to define my sense of self?

passing thoughts

Taking time to **t e a c h** children skills is a building block of self-esteem. I taught my children how to use sharp knives safely as preschoolers. They glowed with satisfaction at being able to chop vegetables or tofu for the family meal. I rarely tell a child, "You're too young to learn that." I find a piece of the job I think they can handle with instruction and **s u p p o r t** and show them how to do that piece. I allow for mistakes and messes, slow, fumbling work, and frustrations. I recognize that I could do the job much faster myself, but that an investment of **t i m e** , patience, and faith now will yield a rich harvest of competence and self-esteem later.   —*Sue Klassen*

We are all fragile, bound to fall under the pervasive power that would tell us we need this toy, this degree, or that job to make us worthy people. We too easily forget that our **w h o l e n e s s** and our joy is a product of relationships. The child in each of us must know first of all that we belong to God and are thus worthwhile beings. Our earliest childhood family **r e l a t i o n s h i p s** model the individual worth that lays the groundwork for resistance of powers that would tell us otherwise.   —*Mary Ann Conrad*

l a u g h i n g means people are enjoying each other. It brings a state of felicity, of delight. You feel glad to be alive and you think, this is it! You just don't need much more than this—a group of friends enjoying each other. But laughter is really an indicator of something more basic: of people accepting each other. You are valued because you are alive, not because of how much money you earn or how big your house is. When we have that sense of being **v a l u e d** , of being connected, we don't live lives of consumerism and ambition. We don't need to prove we have worth.   —*Cecile Andrews*[3]

For us, having children accompany and assist a parent in various tasks in the home, yard, garden, and farm has proven useful in building self-esteem. Of course, whenever possible, delegating **r e s p o n s i b i l i t y** according to their abilities is certainly desirable. For example, when we lived in Brazil, our two boys in elementary school knew that as soon as school was out they were to bring home the cows and calves, to prepare for milking.   —*Anette Eisenbeis*

The girls grew up making a lot of music—giving programs, forming a family performing group that traveled to many churches to present programs, and participating in music at college. I think they felt valued by sharing their **t a l e n t s** ; not necessarily their possession of a lot of things.

—*Christine Purves*

When our children reached the age when they were involved in sports, and enjoying those experiences very much, I collected newspaper clippings from our local newspaper: game schedules, post-game reports, and photos. I interspersed these with a few photos I took myself (including pennants, trophies, awards, etc.) and memories of special individual or team **m o m e n t s** that I had written down, and compiled them into an album. I've done several of these over the years, and they've always been gifts treasured by our children. Perhaps the most valuable aspect of a gift like this is the **a f f i r m a t i o n** value it has, particularly when children hit some of the lower points in their self-esteem, as many do, in the turbulence of being teenagers.   *—Margaret Rempel*

try this

compile an album of your child's accomplishments. Collect photos, game schedules, and written memories of individual or team performances or life milestones.

teach children confidence to be cautious and smart in new situations, not paralyzed by fear.

laugh together! Enjoy each other and the pleasure of just being together.

let children contribute to the job. Encourage them to learn new skills; be patient with mistakes and messes.

share talents by making a space for children to contribute their abilities and new things they are learning. At home, at church, or in the extended family, encourage children to share music, art, knowledge, and games.

build circles of relationships for children. A loving community will give them a sense of identity and belonging.

speak an affirming word to children in your church, extended family or school. Let them know how much you appreciate and enjoy them.

talk about alternative points of view at Thanksgiving, Christmas, whenever school values clash with home values.

give a hug, and receive one too.

listen carefully to children. Notice what children are saying through words and body language. Let them know you understand their feelings even when you disagree.

3.

connecting with others

Ask children to look beyond themselves to their family,
their community, and the world.

There is a boy here who has five barley loaves and two fish.
But what are they among so many people?
—*John 6:9, NRSV*

MEDITATION **simple division**

In our family of three boys, learning to share takes a lot of energy. We divide the last piece of cake into three identical portions, use a timer to take turns on the trampoline, and work out a chore schedule so everyone does an equal amount of work. With an acute sense of justice, our children demand that we intervene when the sharing is not fair.

Recently I realized that we unconsciously have been using two definitions for sharing. Sometimes sharing means dividing what we have into equal portions among ourselves. But we use the same word to describe the times when we give a portion of our abundance to others. I had to admit the existence of two definitions when my son, Ben, showed me a story he had written.

In the story, set in Nigeria, a boy named Michael discovers that his friend Sadik has been stealing clothes from him. My son resolved the conflict in the story by having Michael give Sadik half of his good shirts and half of his play shirts. Sadik reciprocates by giving Michael a wire car. In Ben's mind, the story problem was simple: A boy has six shirts. He decides to share his shirts with a friend. How many shirts does each boy have?

As I read the story, I wondered. Would I have allowed my son to share half of his possessions? The sharing that I preach is not always the sharing I practice. I might have advised him that he could only spare one shirt. My definition of sharing wavers from simple division to a division that only shares the remainder.

Too often my example shows that sharing is what I do with our leftovers. I give away clothes, but only when I've outgrown them. I share garden produce after my freezer overflows. I encourage our children to give away their toys when they accumulate too many to fit on the toy shelf. I volunteer my time when it does not cut into my earning hours. I donate our spare change that I won't miss anyway.

Sharing my excess is good, but it is also pain free and can be done almost without thinking. Where did I get the idea that sharing shouldn't affect me? Ben defined it this way: "Sharing is giving something away that if the other person didn't need it, you would be using it yourself." Sadik gave Michael a wire car that he valued. Justice comes in equalizing the need with what is available. Two boys share six shirts. How many shirts does each boy have?

I struggle with Ben's idea of sharing. Isn't it reckless to give away the clothing that I have carefully provisioned for our family? What about the boy who gave away his loaves and fishes? Didn't he know that if he shared his small lunch among so many people, no one's hunger would be satisfied? Shouldn't I be teaching my children to plan ahead for future needs?

When we lived in Congo, food was shared with unexpected visitors whose arrival coincides with mealtime. We often heard our friends pray, "May God multiply what we have so that what is shared is enough."

—Jeanne Zimmerly Jantzi

With God as the source of our being, we recognize our interdependence on the created world and our connections with others. We want to help children understand their connections with their families, communities, and others around the world.

Children depend on their families to nurture them. They depend on the efforts of many people every day to provide them with the necessities and luxuries of life. Our children depend on the friendship of others to surround and support them. Author Douglas Hall wrote:

The confession that God is the source and ground of our being is . . . a confession of our dependence on these created "others": the parents who conceived and nurtured us; the siblings whose companionship (and rivalry) shaped our formative years; the friends, co-workers, neighbors, teachers, students, and colleagues with whom we are linked in voluntary or involuntary communality; the dogs and cats whose presence in our childhood and at other times may have been even more significant than that of people; the animals and plants that sustain our bodies . . .; the trees, the particular landscapes, the mountains, the sea, the rivers and prairies; the sun and skies; . . . through each and all of these . . . our being has been shaped and is being sustained.[1]

When we consider ourselves part of the web of all creation, we value cooperation, interdependence, and justice. This provides children an alternative view to the individualism and competition of much North American culture.

Children receive constant messages from school, friends, and the media that urge them to look out for number one. Popular North American culture teaches

how can we help children balance their needs with the needs of others?

what opportunities exist in my community to help children connect with others who need a fair share?

children these implicit lessons about the way to be happy:

Wealth is the key to the good life.

We should get what we want when we want it.

Happiness is found in things.

Personal enjoyment is of paramount importance.[2]

What are the effects of looking out for myself in a world of limited resources and unequal distribution of wealth? How can we move ourselves and our children beyond the stage of egocentrism?

"The presence of community is a powerful reminder that authentic wealth does not consist in the size of one's bank account, but in the depth and diversity of relationships within the community: the mechanic who won't overcharge you, the neighbor you can trust your kids with, and the landscape and other creatures so familiar to you that you know you are home."[3]

Contributor Libby Caes wrote:

When we lived in Philadelphia my husband volunteered at least weekly at a free clinic for the homeless. The focus of the clinic was not the delivery of medical care but building relationships. The clinic was a safe and welcoming place for those who came. When our daughter, Amy, was on vacation or had a day off from school, she went with Dave to the clinic. She would sit in the waiting room and do whatever chores needed to be done—making patient charts or counting medicines. Amy would listen to the conversations around her and observe the activity around her as she worked. Among her favorite people were the two women who ran the clinic. She prayed for them nightly.

We can give our children opportunities to both give and receive. Growing up,

who are those different from my family and church in our community? how can we and our children really get to know them?

I experienced two-way connections with others beyond my extended family and cultural community. I saw my parents helping people across cultural and class boundaries, but I also saw my family receiving help from these friends. Our family received many bags of garden produce from James, a disabled veteran who struggled with alcoholism, and Lydie, his mother. Somphit, a Lao friend, sewed traditional Lao clothing for my mother, which she wore with pride. Even these days, Vali, a friend and neighbor to my parents, sometimes brings a meal to their home when they admit to fatigue. My parents modeled the value of reciprocity and the dignity that comes to others when we allow ourselves to be on the receiving end.

We can work at developing relationships across cultural and socioeconomic boundaries. Diverse relationships do not happen by accident. Children form connections based on neighborhoods, schools, and activities, which are often filled with people just like them. Contributor Sue Getman wrote:

When we have an opportunity to do so, we invite people from other countries, or missionaries who are home on leave, to visit with us in our home so that our daughter can learn how people in other parts of the world live. We also try to facilitate relationships and contacts locally with people who have disabilities or people of other races. We are hoping that these practices will help her develop an ability to relate to people from various backgrounds and also root in her a sense of compassion and a concern for justice.

We seek to help our children develop empathy with others, to be able to graciously receive as well as give and to feel the discontent that pulls them to work for justice for all God's creation. Making conscious connections can help children experience the positive synergy of interdependence.

do I accept help from others as well as offering help?
in what ways can children learn to give generously and receive thankfully?

passing thoughts

My extended family has a tradition of volunteering. When we each turned twelve, we were told we were old enough to start volunteering in the community, too. We worked hundreds of **happy** hours doing arts and crafts at nursing homes, assisting the nurses at the blood bank, and playing board **games** with patients at the local trauma recovery hospital. None of these things directly benefitted us or anyone we knew, which made the giving even more gratifying.

—Judith Vargo

Learning to **cook** ethnic meals from people of different cultures has been a wonderful way for our family to broaden our **friendships**. We asked Kalpana, a woman from India with whom my husband works, to help teach us how to cook a traditional Indian meal. Soon ten-year-old Nathan was **flipping** crispy lentil-rice pancakes, called *dosa*, like a pro. Six-year-old Sylvia was delighted to sit cross-legged on the floor and use her fingers instead of cutlery in traditional Indian fashion.   *—Sue Klassen*

When our children were college and high school age, we spent five days over several Christmases helping international students experience Christmas, an otherwise lonely time as libraries and labs are closed at the university and all the other students had gone home. Our children learned to share their lives and have **fun** times with new friends from many countries and **cultures**.

—Arlene Block

One way we visualize our connections with others is with a poster of the earth as seen from space, with no **b o r d e r s** .   —*Michelle Bull*

We want our children to learn to live comfortably with **d i v e r s i t y** . They attend a public school with a socioeconomic and racial mix among classmates. Our choice of living in the city in a huge old house provides the opportunity for us to host people from different places with all sorts of interesting **s t o r i e s** that enrich our lives.   —*Carol Martin Johnson*

Our family volunteered to cook for and serve the homeless at a free lunch program. Instead of waiting in line for the meal, the guests were served at their tables **p e r s o n a l l y** . The boys met and talked with people who had many different life stories.   —*Bobbie Van de Veer*

One Christmas we bought from UNICEF a wonderful book, *Children Just Like Me*, and read about a child each night and looked on the globe to find their country. Reading is a good way to expand **h o r i z o n s** .

—*Mary Ann Conrad*

We try to keep in touch with **r e f u g e e** families living in our community. This not only keeps us aware of personal struggles to live within extremely limited financial boundaries but also **r e m i n d s** us of political struggles and injustices in other parts of the world.   —*Brenda MacDonald*

Last winter I made a **q u i l t** for a person in another country. I did it because I know that there are kids who are not as fortunate as I am. I like to imagine a child **a s l e e p** with the quilt. My mom made me a quilt, and I like to sleep under it when it is cold outside.   *—Brian Martin (age 10)*

If we have **o p p o r t u n i t i e s** to meet people from other countries we try to learn from them and find a way to stay connected. One of our daughters has chosen to use her "gift to God" monies to help support changes happening in South Africa because she heard a South African pastor speak about his life.
                                                                                —James and Aldine Musser

An MCC worker spoke one morning during our worship service about the plight of children in Iraq under sanctions. He so **i n s p i r e d** two eleven-year-old boys, Jonathan and Ryan, that they started a fundraiser and collected more than $150. The next week they asked for time in the service to tell us how they would like to help Iraqi children. We responded because we knew these boys had their **h e a r t s** in the right place and knew their priorities.   *—Lorne Buhr*

Our small group at church took part in a program to house and feed families who are temporarily without **h o m e s**. We all prayed, ate, and played together. Our children directly interacted with other families with children their age who had no homes and were down on their luck. They saw other families just like us trying to stay together, have decent meals, playing the **s a m e g a m e s**. The children enjoyed this interaction.   *—Marie Harnish*

use the news and read a map. Help kids learn about the world as events bring up different countries.

learn to cook ethnic meals from people of different cultures. Invite visitors and members to contribute for a church ethnic food meal.

remember the nuts and bolts. Make a quilt; gather food for a food pantry; pack supplies for emergency relief; pass out meals to the hungry.

open your door to a refugee family in your neighborhood. Listen to their stories. Help children gain compassion and awareness by finding out about refugees' home cultures.

try this

read an international folk tale to children. Ask an international friend to share a story in children's time or Sunday school.

welcome international students for Christmas celebrations.

invite someone you would "never invite to our house" for a meal.

volunteer regularly in your community with children from your family or church. Get to know people in nursing homes, homeless shelters, hospitals, or food pantries.

4.

spending time

Provide children with the elbow room
to develop their passions.

Better is a handful with quiet
      than two handfuls with toil,
   and a chasing after wind.
            —Ecclesiastes 4:6, NRSV

MEDITATION **the pattern of life**

I remember as a child, waking up each morning excited to see what the day would hold. My brother and I cooked up great fun; sometimes we'd plan our futures in the loft in the garage creating awesome possibilities for our friends and ourselves. Other days we'd hike to a nearby quarry and explore. Sometimes we'd read.

Later, days become months and years to rush through in anticipation of a "better" state: being able to drive, being able to date, being able to vote, being on my own. "Don't wish your life away," my dad would say; of course I ignored him. I had all the time in the world.

When I turned 28, my dad sent me a short birthday letter (he rarely wrote): "Don't think of yourself as a year older, but as having one less year in which to do the things you want to do with your life." "How morbid!" I muttered to Herb, a friend who often spent evenings with us doing jigsaw puzzles.

"How wise," was Herb's response.

At that time I was living in Bangladesh, a country with a different view of time. Time there was not segmented into minutes, seconds, even hours, but was rather a fluid flow of events and relationships. Meetings started, for example, when everyone arrived, not when the big hand reached the twelve. One day, I told a Bengali colleague, "Time is money." He was horrified. I regret that we did not finish that exchange; I was never able to find out his analogy for time, but clearly time was not a force that controlled him. Time was his to control, use, and enjoy. Living there for three years, I learned to treasure the same pattern of life. The hands of the clock did not signal the start and stop of visits; the flow of words, feelings, and shared thoughts did.

Then we reentered the United States, where time stopped for no one and the drive to work hard, acquire the good life, succeed, and store up a nest egg for retirement seemed to control everyone. I remember watching friends work frantically at two jobs to pay off a pool they had no time to swim in. People had no time to visit, only time to work or rush from appointment to appointment and back again.

In no time at all, I accelerated my pace so that I too could be a contributing, successful member of the community and the church. I fit more activities into the day; even worse the hours I devoted to work expanded to fit more of my waking hours, crowding out the time I had for fun and recreation. I didn't notice the blur or my tunnel vision because I had my eyes on a goal—the goal of retiring and having time to relax, read, and kick back. I remember telling a sister-in-law: "When I retire, I want to sit in the sun, read, and sleep like a cat."

"Why don't you sit in the sun, and purr, and sleep now? Why wait for retirement to sit in the sun and relax?" she asked.

The final wake-up call came in 1994 when my younger brother, Steve, the one with whom I had created great fantasies and possibilities, died suddenly with no warning. He was a great person at delayed gratification: "As soon as I finish . . ., then I'll have picnics, get married, have fun, and have children," he'd promise me, our family, and himself. I remember his last summer visit with us; we'd had a cookout in the grove of trees behind our house and from our hammocks had watched the sun go down with our two sons and with Steve. As he said good-bye that summer to go back to his extremely demanding job in a city far away, he cried and asked me if I knew how often he dreamed of the time when he like me could enjoy perfect evenings with children of his own.

With his death died the possibility of his enjoying his dreams.

Suddenly, for me, time was limited. I vowed that *every day* I would have a little bit of the good life I was dreaming of. I cut back my hours at work and spent time hiking, having picnics, and reading in the hammock. I started doing things for my family—and even more radically for myself. I'd take a vacation day to read and sit in the sun.

Our boys, now fifteen and seventeen, have somehow absorbed the message. More than once in the past seven years, they have chosen to spend time at home, reading or relaxing, rather than going to one more activity. One night our son Alex decided not to go to a party with his best friends. "I've been away enough this week," he said. "I want to stay home tonight and just be with the family." Nick, I noticed, creates time for health for himself by going into his room and drawing. He too chooses to limit his activities, though he does not always speak about it; we need to notice and honor his signals that enough is enough.

Time is one resource everyone has equally. No one has forty-eight hours in a day. We all have the same amount of time in a day. The discovery that time is limited forced a discovery of time's value. I hope my sons learn the same message, without the trauma.

—Charmayne Denlinger Brubaker

A
CLOSER
LOOK

We like to think we can handle time in the same way we handle money. We often use money words to talk about time—we manage time, save time, waste time, and spend time. We even say time is money. Yet there is no way to earn or borrow more time. Time is a precious, scarce, nonrenewable resource.

Our time choices reveal what we value. Many of us live in the midst of a hectic whirl of children's schedules, work, church, volunteer activities, and family responsibilities. Our culture values this type of productivity. Busyness has become the norm. We are much better at filling our Christmas letters with recitals of what we are *doing* than what we are *being*.

So many good activities, opportunities, and needs surround us that we may be tempted to think we can and should do it all, all of the time. With busy adults as their models, children may also come to believe that their time and energy stretch to infinity.

In my own life, I find it difficult to keep spaces of time open. My children observe a mother who never sits still and who has a hard time just "being." Most of the time I rest only when I am fatigued and unable to do any more. Then I consider Genesis 2:2. God rested on the seventh day from all the work he had done. God did not set aside that day of rest simply to recoup energy to begin creating another universe during the next work week. Resting was valuable in its own right.[1]

Resting requires planning for space in our allotment of time. Theologian Gerald May wrote about the value of spaciousness of time.

what open spaces do the children in my life have?

Space is freedom: freedom from confinement, from preoccupation, from oppression, from drivenness, and from all other interior and exterior forces that bind and restrict our spirits. We need space in the first place simply to realize how compelled and bound we are. Then we need space to allow the compulsions to ease and the bonds to loosen. In the Hebrew sense, our passion needs elbow-room.[2]

We want to provide children with the elbowroom to develop their passions and connections with other people. We want to give them time to wonder at God's creation and to exercise their creative abilities. We need to find ways to free ourselves and our children from the cultural expectation that a person's worth is measured by the tightness of her schedule.

Children need time to experience childhood. At no other point in their lives will children be able to experience so freely the spaciousness of time. Yet parents often try to quickly mold them into timekeepers. Children and adults experience cultural differences when it comes to watching the clock. Many of my own family's conflicts have to do with parents and children having different expectations about time. My children like to "smell the roses" and "live for the moment." I want them to speed up and stop dawdling! Our days need some spaciousness in order to diffuse the tension.

I asked a group of middle schoolers what people needed to be contented. Alison, who was eleven at the time, offered her opinion about cutting down the stress in her life.

What do people need to feel content? No homework, no school, no work. Nothing you have to do now. You know, like hassles. Like you have to get this

how can I help them create or protect open spaces in their lives?

done now. Like you have to run over to piano lessons now, *and you have to go to gymnastics* now.

Children need time to be open to God. It would never work in my active household to schedule a specific time for my boys to sit quietly and listen to God. But when there is a spaciousness of time, children have the freedom to settle into a balanced life of activities and open places. On an "open" day, my children set their own rhythms of activity and quiet.

One morning four-year-old Paul decided to take a break from his busy playing. He sat on the floor soaking up a square of sunshine as I worked at my desk. Suddenly he looked up at me with surprise and asked in a hushed voice, "Did you hear that?" "What?" I asked. "God just talked to me," he said with round eyes.

Arlie Hochschild, a professor at the University of California, believes that time with children cannot be borrowed.

Often parents . . . unwittingly create little debt collectors in their children. In exchange for not being available, . . . they will trade time on an upcoming Saturday for lack of time now. Thus, the family copes with Monday through Friday with the promise of Saturday. The children collect not bills, but love, payable at a later date.[3]

Parents need the spaciousness of time to enjoy each stage of their children's lives. When David was an infant, I sat down in a comfortable rocker in a friend's home to nurse. On the wall beside the chair, my friend had posted a poem. Each stanza named an uncompleted task in the home and restated the poet's decision to ignore the task because "I'm rocking my baby and babies don't keep." As our boys grow into new stages of life, I want to remember the preciousness of each of these stages. Nine-year-olds don't keep either.

An art education instructor once taught me to write a preschooler's name on the back of his artwork or on an attached card. She pointed out that adults often invade a child's artwork by considering any open space to be available space to print the name and date. She explained that open spaces in art are not blank spots, but an important part of the composition. Open spaces in time also deserve our respect. Our children need the spaciousness of their parents' time as well as their own undirected time to wonder, think, create, and enjoy relationships.

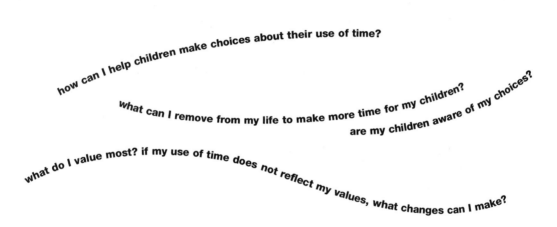

how can I help children make choices about their use of time?

what can I remove from my life to make more time for my children?

are my children aware of my choices?

what do I value most? if my use of time does not reflect my values, what changes can I make?

passing thoughts

I sat on the back porch with my mother and daughter in Montgomery, Alabama, one humid southern summer evening and realized that in just one breath, one **heartbeat** ago, I was in my young daughter's place, sitting with my own mother and grandmother in the damp and fragrant heat. In yet just another breath, another **heartbeat**, I realized as well, I would be in my mother's place, rocking with my own daughter and granddaughter. How quickly time passes. How quickly the chance to practice open-hearted parenting slips through our hands. How precious this brief time we are given with our children truly is. Ask yourself: "If I were to go through one typical day with my children with this tender, bittersweet **awareness** of the fleetness and fragility of time in my heart, how would it change my life as a parent?" —*Melissa West*[4]

Until last year, Dave and I both worked at **home**. Neither of us worked full time. So, we were available. One day Amy came home and remarked that the **fathers** of all her classmates left for work early in the morning and did not return home until after dinner. She was so glad Dave's schedule was not like that. Now I am working full time. Dave has chosen not to seek full-time employment because of Amy. This has limited his career options but I am thankful for his commitment to being **present** in Amy's life while she is still home. We both know that all too soon she will no longer be living with us but will be an independent young adult.

—*Libby Caes*

When our children were young, perhaps six and nine years old, we asked them this question: "What do you think we think is **i m p o r t a n t** ?" After explaining that we simply wanted them to speak from their own observations of our lives, we were quite astonished by the first answer: "Well, it's important to hurry up!" This was certainly not our own perception of what we valued most highly. The second answer was that "It is important to spend time together." This relieved our anxieties a bit. Try this exercise . . . you may learn some **s u r p r i s i n g** things!   —*Titus Peachey*

I learned from my neighbor, MuaMbuyi, in Congo to come outside and sit. When **v i s i t o r s** came, she would come outside and allow the curtain covering her door to swing shut behind her, closing off any busyness in the house. She would bring chairs out to the **s h a d e** of the mango tree and focus on the visitors at hand.   —*Jeanne Zimmerly Jantzi*

Some Sunday evenings we ban anything with a screen (television, computer, video games, etc.) and instead play games together. This family time has provided us with time to visit, time to have **f u n** together, time to think and learn. The children look forward to and value this time.   —*Kelli Burkholder King*

ask your children if their schedules are too full. Which activities are most important to them? How much free time do they want? What can they drop or change to accomplish this?

try a no TV evening one night a week. Shut off TV, videos, and computer and play a game or do an activity together.

try this

think outside the box. Look at other families and their choices; are some right for you?

plan open family time ahead, write it down and don't fill it with other things.

listen to children's ideas and encourage creativity when "I'm bored" rears its head. Slow down and enjoy the moment. Choose to spend time with children, enjoying each stage of their lives.

involve children in decisions about time use. When the decision must be an adult's, talk with children about why you made the choice you did.

what is important to us? Ask your children this question. If their answers don't match what you believe is important, decide what changes can make your life reflect your beliefs.

just say no! Decide how many activities or events to be involved with in a week, then decline all offers beyond that.

think big. When you look back someday over your life and the lives of children you are involved with, what do you hope to have done, accomplished, and enjoyed with them?

get rid of things. If possessions are a factor in workload, stress, and time shortage, make a commitment to reduce them by a percentage over the coming year.

live small. Reduce housework by living in no more space than you really need.

5.

caring for creation

Nurture in children a joy in caring for God's creation.

For the creation waits with eager longing
for the revealing of the children of God.
—*Romans 8:19, NRSV*

MEDITATION **fertile ground for wonder**

Our four children love being read to. The worlds created by good storytellers are fertile ground for the seeds of wonder and imagination. Our children also love walking in the woods with their mother, a first-rate naturalist who knows the names of almost every plant and animal we might encounter. Children love reading and children love the creation for the same reason: both are invitations to wonder.

The personification of the natural world always has fascinated children. We have been enamored with the idea that plants, animals, and creatures of all sorts might at some level think, talk, feel, and express emotions. From *Aesop's Fables* to *Charlotte's Web*, from the *Chronicles of Narnia* to *The Phantom Toll Booth*, the human imagination has ascribed characteristics of personhood to plants and animals. The *Beastes*, a book popular during the Middle Ages, personified a whole catalog of creatures to teach children practical ethics.

In the Bible, we again find the personification of the creation. We find that not only redeemed persons feel great joy in their redemption, the redeemed creation too shares this joy. "The desert and the parched land will be glad; the wilderness will rejoice and blossom" (Isa. 35:1, NIV). "The mountains and hills will burst into song before you, and all the trees of the field will clap their hands" (Isa. 55:12, NIV).

It is not just humanity that languishes under the effects of sin and suffering. "Because of this [sin] the land mourns, and all who live in it waste away; the beasts of the field and the birds of the air and the fish of the sea are dying" (Hos. 4:3, NIV).

Jesus himself tells us that if the crowds had been kept at bay the stones themselves would have cried out in praise when he rode into Jerusalem. Children can understand these truths better than the rest of us. Their minds are still clear and untainted by adult realism. Stones cry out, hills burst into song, trees clap their hands, wilderness rejoices; these are not just poetic expressions to the mind of a child, but statements that resonate in their minds as literally true.

The creation itself truly suffers under the effects of human arrogance, ignorance, and greed. Yet the creation rejoices as its redemption draws near. The apostle Paul tells us that "the creation waits with eager longing for the revealing of the children of God" (Rom. 8:19, NRSV) It stands on tiptoes, it has its neck outstretched, it strains to see, it is eager and expectant. (This paraphrase comes from Fr. Gregoria, a theologian from India.)

Because Christ has replaced our arrogance with humility, our greed with giving, our ignorance with loving knowledge, we are God's children, the people the world is waiting for. The creation truly suffers and creation can truly be glad. Children can imagine this. Creation is eagerly longing for the children of God to be revealed.

—*Rob Cahill*

I love hearing five-year-old Paul breathe, "Beeaauutiful!" as he discovers some new wonder outdoors. Paul can be passionate about almost everything he sees. Why do I always try to hurry him when he prefers to amble along and examine each thing that interests him? Our children help us rediscover the wonder and mysteries of God's creation. They approach life with expectancy, enthusiasm, curiosity, and awe.

When our family lived in Nigeria, we took a camping trip with some other American mission workers. Our children spent a wonderful weekend swimming, climbing rocks, and playing. On the way home, we followed the other family along the winding, rutted road. As we rounded a corner, we had to brake abruptly behind the lead car. We saw our friend dumping their baby's disposable diapers into a ravine. Our children took in the scene and fell into a shocked silence. Finally David blurted out in confusion, "But I thought he was a Christian!" To David, the connection was clear; our care for creation is an expression of our faith.

Children catch on to their parents' view of creation whether or not it is stated. Wesley Granberg Michaelson quotes a letter from a friend living on the Lakota Indian reservation in South Dakota:

When most Christians talk about being good stewards of the earth, what they have in mind is something like this: We conserve resources so we can use them in the future, and we conserve some wildlife areas so we can admire and enjoy their beauty. I don't think this is biblically sound because both of these ideas are still caught up in human idolatry. The creation exists for the welfare of the human race in this thinking. I don't believe that, I think we are all part of the entire creation,

read Romans 8:19-22.
how do we share our liberation with the rest of the creation?

with our own unique roles, and we exist for God. . . .

We are all in relationship with one another because we are all in relationship with God. . . . The Lakota people have an elaborate kinship system (including) the earth, who is your grandmother, the sky and eagle, who are your brothers. When you think circular like this you place prime importance on right and proper relationships. You don't abuse or use your relatives, human or otherwise.[1]

Do we see humans as the centerpiece of the world and consider all of creation in relation to us? Or do we see God at the center and everything that God created in relationship to God? Jewish people at the time of Christ recognized two categories in the world: "the Creator and that which the Creator fashions. So humans, animals, plants, and rocks all belong to the same category: creation."[2] This view does not eliminate the caretaker role of humans. It simply removes humans from center stage and acknowledges that all God's creation exists for God. Would thinking of God at the center of creation change the way we talk with children about creation care? How might it affect our behavior?

When we see ourselves as part of the vast and intricate system that the Creator has made, we begin to understand our interdependence with creation. Caring for creation is about preserving for future generations, cooperating with nature's processes, and living in harmony with others. It is about working toward God's purposes. We begin to make the leaps, links, and connections to see how all of creation is gloriously intertwined with God in the center.

If we consider humans the center of creation, we may assume that all creation acts with self-interest. We may see nature in a competitive survival of the fittest. Do we see creation as competitive or as cooperative? Biologist Lewis Thomas states,

when have I witnessed the suffering of creation?

when have I experienced creation rejoicing?

A century ago there was a consensus about this: nature was "red in tooth and claw," evolution was a record of open warfare among competing species, the fittest were the strongest aggressors, and so forth. Now it begins to look different. . . . The urge to form partnerships, to link up in collaborative arrangements, is perhaps the oldest, strongest, and most fundamental force in nature. There are no solitary, free-living creatures, every form of life is dependent on other forms.[3]

God has given humans of all sizes the unique job of being caretakers of God's creation. This is a concrete act of faith for both adults and children. Contributor Michelle Bull wrote:

We feel that if we foster a real appreciation of God's creation in our children they will be filled with awe, and that will make it easier for them to feel awe before God, and gratitude toward God. At a very young age, kids are quite concrete. Later they can understand abstract things better. By experiencing awe and wonder, I feel it will be easier for them to grasp some of the concepts of God when they're old enough truly to understand.

We can help children respond concretely to the Creator. When our creativity brings love and beauty into the world, we act as our maker's image. We also bring the image of the Creator more clearly into focus in the world.[4] Instead of being motivated by guilt and fear over the future of human beings, we care for God's creation because it belongs to God and God made it good. God is at the center of our motivation.

how do I see children responding to God's creation? what can I learn from them?

passing thoughts

We have tried to nurture a love of nature in Lydia. When she showed interest when I watered the plants, I let her help, and she has spent a lot of time outside with her cup and bucket, watering plants. She digs in the **garden** when I work in the garden. I watch **bugs** when she watches bugs. She also helps clean up inside—some things go in the trash can, some into the recycling bag, and some into the compost bucket. Care of God's environment and love of God's nature are a part of our faith that she can **touch** and see.

—*Winnie Brubaker Haggard*

We find that outdoor family time is essential. We talk about reverence, interconnectedness, and the sacredness of life. As an aid we have built a **campfire** ring in our backyard. It has hundreds of small (and not so small) stones from our travels and family milestones. Friends from afar also add rocks. It is the place where we remind ourselves of the joys of those travels and the lessons learned. It is where we start trips and undertakings with prayer and where we reconvene upon return. It's our small piece of the **sacred** .   —*Dennis Boyer*

A Winnebago Indian mother suggested to us several years ago that we spend **quiet** time with our children outside, not "doing" anything, not even walking, just being there and listening and thinking. We have just begun to try to do this with the children, especially with one child at a time.

—*James and Kathleen McGinnis*[5]

Each of the children have a small plot in our garden in which they plant their favorite foods. Last year Peter said he wanted to plant **p i z z a** . We planted everything that goes on a pizza (except for the wheat and cheese). When it was all ripe Peter helped harvest and prepare his pizza. He even got to make the mozzarella cheese for the topping. We called it Peter's Pizza Garden.

—Rob Cahill

We are careful about environmental issues, and the kids see us practicing what we preach, and also discussing it in global terms. We point out to them that the reason we have acid rain, and some of our **l a k e s** (where we like to canoe) are dying, is because we live downwind from the Eastern Seaboard of the United States, so that what happens in one place affects other places. Or they ask why we use rags to clean things up, not **p a p e r t o w e l s**, and we remind them of the clear-cuts we've seen lately, and explain that those are necessary to make paper towels.   *—Michelle Bull*

A **c a b b a g e** was not something common and heavy at the bottom of a supermarket shopping cart, but a special gift the family had tended and protected from deer and dry weather. How clear, after many years, is the memory of the **t r i u m p h a l** march of our four children as they carried a choice cabbage up the staircase, through the front room, and into the kitchen. That was certainly no ordinary vegetable; it was a beautiful, variegated green orb, a precious trophy!

—John C. Wiebe

One of the first household chores that our son took on as a three-year-old was emptying our **c o m p o s t** bucket out in the appointed spot in the yard. An easy task that made him feel useful, and provided a chance to talk about why we don't just put that stuff in the trash can.   —*Andrea Schrock Wenger*

Develop a **h o b b y** that takes you outside, and whose object is getting to know the inexhaustible variety of creation. Bird watching; pressing wildflowers; identifying trees, shrubs, and mosses; growing **g e r a n i u m s** , gladiolas, or dahlias; these hobbies take a minimum of equipment.

—*Loren and Mary Ruth Wilkinson*[6]

We want our children to live joyfully and find joy in the everyday—the moon-flower we planted that sports **s p e c t a c u l a r** fragrant white flowers every day after dark. The yellow rose bush that is **b l o o m i n g** in the tiny yard in front of the row home we pass on the walk home from school; planting seeds and picking tomatoes, green beans, and cucumbers from our small plot in a community garden that came into being on the site of a former abandoned apart-ment building.   —*Carol Martin Johnson*

try this

give each child a small plot in the garden to plant their favorite foods.

empty the compost with your child. Use the chance to talk about trash or the cycle of nature.

let children contribute by soliciting their ideas when making family or church decisions that affect the environment.

get dirty together. Let children work in the garden with you; examine bugs, plants, and animals together.

find joy in everyday creation: flowers, stargazing, gardening, the phases of the moon, the change of the seasons.

include God in the conversation when you talk about the environment with children. Talk about how people are caretakers of God's creation.

slow down and rediscover the wonder of God's creation. Learn from children and examine nature with curiosity, enthusiasm, and awe.

make a campfire ring with stones from travels, family milestones, and friends far away. Use it as a place to start and end trips and undertakings with prayer.

develop outside hobbies: birdwatching, pressing wildflowers, and identifying trees. Encourage children to participate.

talk about the environmental choices you make and why. Don't assume children will know the reasons for your actions.

**spend quiet
time outside** with a child, just being there, and listening and thinking.

help sense your family's connections with God's creation in the place where you live. Find the answers to this list of questions from Loren and Mary Ruth Wilkinson's book, *Caring for Creation in Your Own Backyard*.

1. Trace the water you drink from precipitation to tap.

2. How many days until the moon is full? (plus or minus a few days?)

3. Describe the soil around your house.

4. What were the primary subsistence techniques of the culture(s) that lived in your area before you?

5. Name five native edible plants in your area and their season(s) of availability.

6. From what directions do winter storms generally come in your area?

7. Where does your garbage go?

8. How long is the growing season where you live?

9. Name five trees in your area. Are any of them native?

10. Name five resident and five migratory birds in your area.

11. What is the land use history by humans in your area during the past century?

12. What primary geological event or process influenced the landform where you live?

13. From where you are reading this, point north.

14. What spring wildflower is consistently among the first to bloom where you live?

15. What kinds of rocks and minerals are found in your area?

16. How many people live next door to you? What are their names?

17. How much gasoline do you use in a week, on the average?

18. What developed and potential energy resources are in your area?

19. What plans are there for large development in your area?

20. What is the largest wild region in your area?[7]

6.

managing money

Talk explicitly with children about the place of money
and the place of God in our lives.

Do not say to yourself,
"My power and the might of my own hand have gotten me this wealth."
But remember the Lord your God,
for it is he who gives you power to get wealth,
so that he may confirm his covenant that he swore to your ancestors,
as he is doing today.
—*Deuteronomy 8:17-18, NRSV*

MEDITATION   **graceful allowance**

We give our children a weekly allowance of money. Allowance is free, our children do not have to earn it, but we do require certain patterns of using the money. We divide it into four parts which our five- and seven-year-old sons put into jars labeled "Offering," "Helping Others," "College," and "Mark" or "Ben" (personal spending money). They have discovered a sense of empowerment in this allowance agreement. They are able to join in offering during worship, purchase items for Sunday school giving projects, earn interest on college funds, and buy a toy they want.

Allowance is more than just a Saturday routine. It is a reflection of God's gift of grace, rooted in the covenant relationship God established with the children of Israel. In that "allowance agreement" God lavished goodness upon the people: deliverance from slavery, protection and sustenance in the wilderness, and a homeland flowing with water, food, and natural resources. God generously provided for the needs of the people, but warned them not to forget the source of this blessing. This wealth was not the product of their own labor, but the fruit of a covenant initiated by God.

According to the dictionary, meanings for the word "allowance" include: "an allotted share," "money given regularly as a bounty," and "the taking into account of mitigating circumstances." When it comes to money, parents take into account their children's immaturity and lack of earning power, and give them a head start on economic viability by providing allowance. In the spiritual realm, God takes into account our sin and yet extends grace to us. It is out of that experience of grace that we grow into people of mature faith.

Sometimes we forget that money ultimately comes as a gift, not a paycheck. Even when we "earn" money we do so using skills and strength from God. Children must learn to earn and manage money in the context of gratitude and generosity. The relationships we build with children are the covenants in which they develop responsibility born of grace, guided by these principles of faithful financial stewardship:

Acknowledge our human needs and trust God to meet those needs, not hoarding money or worrying about getting more of it.

Do not seek money as an end in itself, but as a resource to be used for God's purposes in the world, according to God's standards of justice and peace.

Receive gratefully, manage carefully, and share joyfully what God has given.

—David and Heidi Kreider Regier

many families use allowances to their children to develop the mechanics of faithful money management. There are two ways of thinking about allowances. Some families tie allowance to doing household chores, while other families give allowance to their children just because they are members of the family.

A "just because" allowance assumes that everyone helps in the smooth operation of the household just because they belong to the family. If children neglect their chores, they lose privileges, rather than money. While tying allowance to chores may help children learn the value of work, it could turn the family into a marketplace where payment is required for services rendered.

Children are developmentally ready to understand the concept of money and allowances at age six or seven. Together, families must discuss what the allowance will cover—clothes? lunch money? entertainment? As children grow older some families give a larger allowance and expect children to manage their clothing purchases or other expenses. Managing allowance money enables children to practice giving, saving, and wise spending.

David Walsh, a psychologist who focuses on parenting issues, suggests that parents need to remain involved in children's money decisions. "It's not the responsibility of children to set boundaries and limits for themselves. Parents have to set the limits to maintain balance. With all the marketing aimed at kids, how can we help them to resist?"[1] We are only able to help our children resist marketing if we are consistent in our own lives.

For the most part, books that connect faith and finances focus on what we do

when did I receive money for the first time in my life? was it a gift, or was it "earned"?

with our money. In *A Christian View of Money*, Mark Vincent states: "Our use of money tells others about our worldview."[2] It is clear that our giving, debt, investing, savings, and planning all reflect our faith.

Many people show children how to pay bills, balance a checkbook, calculate a tithe, and open a savings account. They talk with their children about faithful giving and good stewardship of money. Vicki Robin and Joe Dominguez, in *Your Money or Your Life*, call this the practical, physical realm of money.[3]

Unfortunately, we often limit ourselves to this practical realm. Money is often seen as a fact of life and children's allowance as a rite of passage into the mysteries of the "real world." In truth, our faith and money connections happen in a larger arena than this practical, physical realm.

If our faith and money discussions with children focus on only the mechanics of giving, we miss out on the spirit of worship, of gracious generosity, and of concern for others. Jesus is owner of all our life, not just 10 percent of our money.

By limiting our discussions with children to the practical, physical realm, they may get the impression money will solve most problems. How do you get an expensive toy you really want? Save or earn more money. How will we help those who are poor? Send them money. How will we prepare for the future? Save more money. How will we meet our needs? Earn plenty of money.

Money is not the source of our security, acceptance, power, or personal worth. All these things come from God, who is Lord of our whole lives. The core of the faith and finances discussion is not so much about money, but about our use of our lives. Dominguez and Robin wrote:

Money is something we chose to trade our life energy for. Our life energy is

how was allowance handled in my home?

our allotment of time here on earth, the precious hours available to us . . . while money has no intrinsic value, our life energy does—at least to us. It's tangible . . . It's precious because it is limited and irretrievable and because our choices about how we use it express the meaning and purpose of our life here on earth.[4]

What would happen if we did not narrowly focus on money but included it in thinking of the faithful use of the lives God has given us? We can model for children a way to think critically about what money means to us, to trust in God, and to give freely in response to God's generosity.

how do I balance the values of grace (giving money, nurturing generosity) and responsibility (encouraging the earning and saving of money) in talking with children about money?

when is money a blessing from God? when is money a curse?

do I talk about money with children beyond the practical realm of saving, spending, tithing, or planning? are my attitudes about money ones I want children to share? if not, what can I change?

passing thoughts

We gave our two teenagers a whole year's allowance in one installment on their birthdays. That's all there was for clothing and entertainment for the year. The point was to teach personal responsibility, **p r i o r i t i e s** , consequences of choices, and to cut down on the humiliation of "begging." Retraction of one's allowance could not be used as a punishment. Our daughter Elysha had a rough time the first year. She spent it all too quickly. She did much **b e t t e r** the following years. Son Peter never learned how to save. He had a job and spent it all on his car and girlfriend. Then in his senior year of high school he said, "You know, Dad, if you don't spend so much, you don't have to make so much." He finally got it!
—Gerald and Rita Iversen

Making a **b u d g e t** can also be a way of acting out a sense of stewardship: good stewards are accountable for what has been given to them. Keeping a careful accounting of precisely where money goes is a struggle (efficient record-keeping not being a strong point for either one of us), but we are working on it. And we see a need to involve our children in it. Other parents have told us that they have successfully **i n v o l v e d** their children in budget discussions, and that their children's attitude toward money and the spending of it changed significantly as the children became more aware of how much things cost and where the money went. They became more responsible about their own spending.
—Kathleen and James McGinnis[5]

When my six-year-old began receiving allowance, his weekly four quarters would go into an allowance box with four separate compartments: SAVE—SHARE—SPEND—CHOOSE. We've talked about what each section means, and each has proven full of learning. **s p e n d :** He can spend this essentially as he chooses. He learns about choices and limits (if I buy this, I can't buy that). **s a v e :** Watching money accumulate that is off-limits for immediate spending is exciting for a child. **s h a r e :** My child gets to choose when and with whom to share these resources. **c h o o s e :** One quarter goes into the slot the child chooses, teaching the idea of discretionary funds with the freedom and responsibility of choice. As people of faith, we teach our children about sharing a portion of our money, challenging ourselves to look at our own **p a t t e r n s** of giving. We take a stand that detaches us in part from the frenzied consumption of our society, and we learn anew the joy of giving through the smile on the child's face as the quarter in hand is lovingly shared with others.   *—Liz Andress*

I'm sure sometimes I say, "You can't have that because we can't afford it." I don't want to say that because I don't want to enforce this notion of scarcity that creates fear in children and in all of us. What I like to talk about is **c h o i c e s** . Because we have chosen to do this with our financial resources, we will not be doing that.   *—Killian Noe*[6]

When we got the **g a m e** of Monopoly, Matthew was about four years old. I have never liked the game (I always lost to a shrewd brother) but like it even less now as I try to live a simple life and share these values with my children. One night as we played the game, it became evident that I was going to be bankrupt quickly and out of the game. Matthew, although not the richest player in the game, began to offer me money. He kept enough to remain solvent, but tried to give me enough to keep me playing too.   —*Carol Loeppky*

As our children manage their allowances, we are learning to know our children better: Benjamin **diligently** saves money to buy more expensive items such as a pocketknife or skateboard; Mark is eager to buy whatever he sees with whatever money he has available, yet he is **generous** in sharing what he buys. Whatever their personalities, Mark and Benjamin are developing stewardship patterns that we hope will remain for the rest of their lives, as they learn that all money is really God's money.   —*David and Heidi Regier Kreider*

try this

encourage children to tithe their earnings.

suggest dividing weekly allowances into "sharing," "saving," and "spending" or similar categories. Label a box for this purpose.

talk about why your family has made certain financial choices. Don't assume children will know.

talk about money as a reflection of God's grace. Explain to children how God provides for us and we pass along his gifts to others.

involve children in family or church budget discussions. Let them see where money goes and why, and solicit their opinions.

teach children about wealth and poverty. Be sure they understand these are not only a result of personal choices, and that our choices affect others' lives.

**write down
what money means**
to you. Write what you
want it to mean to your
children. Do the lists
match? What needs
to change if not?

**make money
part of stewardship
discussions—**
stewardship of talents,
of money, of creation,
of our lives.

7.

shopping

Teach children by words and example to be
conscientious shoppers.

Why do you spend your money
for that
which is not bread,
and your labor
for that
which does not satisfy?
—Isaiah 55:2, NRSV

MEDITATION **favorite things**

ast year on Mother's Day, Laura, my eleven-year-old daughter, outlined what she likes about me: (1) you make great food! (2) you read great stories! (3) you take me shopping! Each item involves an investment of time rather than money. When I take my children's preferences into account, they don't pick at what I cook. They are happy with pancakes and scrambled eggs, spaghetti and pizza, and plain good bread. I was amazed that my bookworm daughter listed the stories I read. She can easily read books for herself. But when we read together, we cuddle on the bed and stop and discuss the ideas in the books and reflect on our values.

Ah, but shopping! Have I failed when one of my daughter's favorite activities is spending money with me in malls? After consideration, I realized that this is one of the few times we are alone together, since the males in our family hate to shop. She doesn't beg for things she doesn't need. She just likes being out and about. Being in the midst of more than enough often gives us a chance to talk about our values. "Oh, Laura, look at this lovely sweater!" "But Mom, we don't need clothes that expensive." "What do you think of this dress?" "Didn't you notice it needs to be dry cleaned?"

My children sometimes beg for more material things. But when they think about what matters most, they want my time, to eat together, read books, or wander about. During these times we discuss our response to Jesus' call to life.

—Susan Mark Landis

a reported 70 percent of all adults visit a regional shopping mall weekly.[1] Shopping has become more than a recreational activity for most people. Our culture tries to convince us that spending is part of the rights and responsibilities of citizenship. We are more often referred to as consumers than as citizens. We are urged to buy to grow the economy, to support our nation's laborers, and to promote democracy. While "self-discipline may be healthy for an individual person, it is not a value in a system promoting acquisitions and excess."[2]

In the post-World War II age of affluence, United States retailing analyst Victor Lebow proclaimed,

Our enormously productive economy . . . demands that we make consumption our way of life, that we convert the buying and use of goods into rituals, that we seek our spiritual satisfaction, our ego satisfaction, in consumption. . . . We need things consumed, burned up, worn out, replaced, and discarded at an ever increasing rate."[3]

In what way does our shopping communicate our faith to children? Do we show them that their worth comes from being children of Creator God, not from what they own?

Tom Atlee describes the following eight patterns of consumption in his article, "The Conversion of the American Dream."[4] Most people do not fit in any one category, but exhibit varying patterns of consumption.

Addicted consumers. We shop to make us feel better or to fill an emptiness inside. On any evening, the mall may be filled with aimless wanderers.

how do I involve children in shopping trips?

Robotic consumers. Advertising or product placement in stores compels us to buy specific things or accept certain ideas without question.

Status-driven consumers. People believe self-worth and importance depends on possessions.

Smart shoppers. Shoppers hunt for bargains, sales, yard sales, and thrift stores. They read *Consumer Reports* and get the best quality for the best price.

Appreciative consumers. Possessions have beauty, craftsmanship, or reflect who we are. We are selective in our consumption.

Self-concerned consumers. We buy what is good for us. We try to learn how products could help or harm our family's health.

Socially responsible consumers. We are motivated by the effect our shopping decisions have on other people and the environment.

Life-engaged shoppers. We shop in order to buy things that we need—any more than that gets in the way.

When our lives are in balance, shopping becomes a necessary task but not a central focus. Most people profess to believe that money cannot buy happiness. However, if we were to calculate the amount of time each week that we devote to shopping, the hours spent earning money with which to buy things, and the hours spent maintaining the things we buy, we may find possessions a more central focus in our lives than we would like.

Children need time to think and dream, to learn how to be creators rather than only consumers. Our culture's commitment to acquiring possessions is only a distraction.

We can help children think of borrowing, repairing, or making something as an alternative to shopping. We can talk with them about the real costs of manu-facturing: environmental costs and costs to other people. We can help children think critically so that they can make their own decisions in a world filled with advertising. One's life does not consist in the abundance of possessions (Luke 12:15).

what standards help me decide how much is enough?

does my faith influence how I shop? how?

how can I use shopping to share and teach my values to my children?

passing thoughts

We limit the times we shop and we go with a list. We study the sales and **c o m p a r e** them with other sales. We become familiar with sale patterns and know when certain items will be put on sale. We learn about the quality of sale products.   —*Ruth Clark*

We always did grocery shopping as a family. Visiting the local farmers' market is a **t r e a t** . Children can be introduced to new vegetables and fruits, meet the growers, learn that it is economical to buy and can or freeze your own food, and as a result you can eat a better diet. On vacation we always visit the local or state markets and stop at **r o a d s i d e** stands where farmers are selling.
                                             —*Wanda Colton*

When our daughter reached the age when peer pressure made her want certain clothes, shoes, etc., I gave her a clothing allowance so I would feel more removed from watching her buy overpriced "status" t-shirts, etc. When she asks my advice, I offer my thoughts but then let her make the **d e c i s i o n s** . This seems to work well for both of us.   —*Amarette Cummings*

We **p l a n** ahead for many purchases that aren't a necessity. We talk about how much an item costs, how it fits into our family budget, whether it contributes to our family's values, and what sort of environmental impact it has (can it be recycled when worn out?).   —*Kelli Burkholder King*

Discussion is key at our house. Our daughter asked one night, "Why is it that the more I have, the more I want?" The fact that she **r e c o g n i z e d** materialism within herself is a good start.   —*Maureen Kehler*

When we first moved to Philadelphia we lived around the corner from The Second Mile Center, a thrift store that gave job skills to unemployed persons. When Amy was an infant, I would often take her over there in the stroller and hunt for **b a r g a i n s** . The practice continued after we moved to a different neighborhood. We **d i s c o v e r e d** new thrift stores. One of our favorite mother-daughter outings was Saturday trips to these stores. We try to buy as much of our clothing as we can in thrift stores. If Amy sees something that she really likes but may not need, we usually buy it.   —*Libby Caes*

I feel that I have been a little too vocal about the pressures to go shopping and buy unnecessary stuff when I hear my younger children's comments to their aunt about **w a n t i n g** things "all fancy." I grew up with 1 Timothy 6:6-8. "Of course, there is great gain in godliness combined with **c o n t e n t m e n t** ; for we brought nothing into the world, so that we can take nothing out of it; but if we have food and clothing, we will be content with these" (NRSV). Now that our teen "needs" to be fashionable, we talk a lot more about the pressures to buy, and allow him to spend money on things that we think are wasteful. We wonder if the messages get through, until he brings home insightful essays—quoting us—written in English class.   —*Carol Bixler*

We do our grocery shopping at the store with the lowest prices; we buy generic brands; we sometimes buy in **b u l k** , if that is less expensive. We plant a garden and eat **f r e s h** produce all summer and have plenty of tomatoes to dry and to make tomato sauce. When time permits, I bake our bread. We do not purchase convenience foods; they are expensive and usually not as healthy as food made from scratch. We taught all our children how to **c o o k** so they do not have to be dependent on fast foods or convenience foods.   *—Linda Price*

I think I have all I **n e e d** . I just **w a n t** a bunch more stuff.

—Lara, age 13

try this

think critically about advertising. Teach children to do the same. Talk about TV and magazine ads, how they work, whether they are deceptive.

encourage community relationships by frequenting smaller stores with your children and getting to know local staff.

give a clothing allowance. Offer advice and opinions but let your child make the choices.

count the cost, not just the money. Think about environmental costs, labor abuses, or other hidden costs when examining prices.

shop conscientiously with your children. Make a list and follow it instead of directionless shopping.

pause and think twice with your child about why you are buying an item. Is it a need or has habit or advertising made it seem necessary when it isn't?

affirm children. If self-worth and status are bad reasons to shop, let your children know they are important and loved for themselves, as they are.

discuss purchases before buying: can we afford it, does it fit our values? Make sure children are involved in the discussion.

borrow, repair, or make something. Help children think of these ideas when the "I want" refrain begins.

teach children how to cook. Encourage learning about healthy food and the various costs of convenience food.

tell Jesus stories about possessions. If your values are rooted in the Bible, make sure those stories and sayings become part of your children's lives too.

give each child $2 to spend on nutritious food each time you go grocery shopping. Use the occasion to talk about nutrition, value, and choice.

bring home a rock to commemorate a trip with children, instead of buying throwaway souvenirs. Paint on the place name and date with nail polish.

relax. Children need the freedom to make bad choices sometimes, and to make different choices from you. Wait a few years, you may be surprised at the values they have learned from you.

show children how to save personal spending money to buy something they really want.

8.

deciding about television

Guide children to be aware of television's access
to our time.

If any of you is lacking in wisdom,
ask God, who gives to all generously and ungrudgingly,
and it will be given you.
—James 1:5, NRSV

MEDITATION **urgent wisdom needed**

I have a love/hate relationship with my television. I love my television when I can watch the news, mystery programs, or literary dramas. I am a supporter of Canadian television and enjoy the documentaries, comedies, and dramas produced here. I am a bit of a news junkie, even though I work in the communications field and know that stories are never truly objective.

I hate my television when I see its effect on my family. My son wants to watch cartoons where good triumphs over evil by beating the tar out of it. My husband watches every known sport and then watches the sports commentary on what he just watched. Both become so completely involved in what they are watching that it is nearly impossible to get their attention if the TV is on.

Of course, this never happens to me. I don't waste my television viewing time. My motives are pure. I only watch good, quality shows and I have control over myself at all times.

Yeah, right.

I have had many discussions about television. Some think of it as an evil thing because of the preponderance of sex and violence in programming and the consumerism it promotes. Some think of it as a great tool on which we can watch videos and programs of our own choice. Some don't think about it at all—it's just there, everywhere, a part of our everyday lives. I wonder what James would say.

The book of James is essentially a book about wisdom. "If any of you is lacking in wisdom, ask God, who gives to all generously" (1:5, NRSV). That wisdom is to guide our decisions about how we handle trials and temptations, how we treat each other, how we talk and listen, and how we pray. The wisdom that comes from God is "pure . . . peace-loving, considerate, submissive, full of mercy and good fruit, impartial and sincere" (3:17, NIV). How does that wisdom guide our decisions about television?

Many people don't seem to think that much about TV until they have children. This is certainly true of my experience. My son makes viewing choices that I don't like because of their violent content. Advertising influences him to such a degree that he associates happy faces with Wal-Mart and can sing most commercial jingles at the drop of a hat. Suddenly TV isn't just there; it is an issue. So what is the wisdom here?

I struggle with the effects TV has on my family. I must also question the wisdom of my own decisions around television. Perhaps the real issue is that television is so commonplace in North American society that we have simply stopped thinking about it and just accept it like we accept computers, telephones, and vehicles—all of which have the capability to influence our lives for good or evil. What would change if we started thinking about how all technology influences us personally? Perhaps then our prayers for wisdom would become more urgent.

—*Angelika Dawson*

A
CLOSER
LOOK

ost of us cannot ignore television. We must make some decisions about what our response will be to this ever-present reality. Will we have one or not have one? If we choose to have one, will we put limits on it? What will our limits be?

Nicholas Johnson, former head of the Federal Communications Commission, pointed out TV's influence on children. "All television is educational. The question is, what does it teach?"[1]

Children learn about life and the world through observing and imitating what they see, even if they see it on a television screen. In many cases the messages of television contradict the God-centered capacities we want to help children develop.

While most parents want their children to learn to resolve conflicts and differences peacefully, television, movie, and video game makers do not necessarily share these values. With so many things competing for children's attention, television programming and advertisers have discovered that violence still gets noticed. As children become desensitized by the numbers of violent acts they see, the level of violence must accelerate in order to hold their attention.

While we want our children to develop connections to others, television subtly reinforces the stereotyping of groups of people. Children pick up the standard character types of the ugly bad guy, the evil Asian villain, the dumb blonde, the Latino gang member, and the goofy nerd. The story lines of commercials and programming can reinforce gender stereotyping.

As we help children learn to give and receive freely rather than focusing on

what kind of television programs do my children enjoy? why?

possessions, television depicts "upbeat, beautiful people immersed in the pursuit of their personal ambitions and surrounded by material goods. This is the image that sells. . . . Our children are not learning about balance, they are learning the values of the marketplace: get what you want and get it now."[2]

What can we do about the conflicting messages television gives children? Realizing the influence of television as a values educator, we need to respond. Some choose to eliminate television completely. Others allow children to view certain types of programs and help their children to watch TV critically.

Children who watch long hours of television gain much of their information about the world from the screen. We can encourage children to experience the world directly, to see everyday things in new and different ways, to have the confidence to imagine freely and not to conform unthinkingly.

We can encourage children to be creative by giving them time: television-free hours and days. Talk with children about the messages of advertising and of television programs. Watch television purposefully. Help children to be joyfully different by being mindful about television's access to our thinking spaces.

whether your children watch TV at home or elsewhere,
how have you seen it influencing them?

am I content with my family's decisions about television? if not, what would I like to change?

how do the problems and benefits of television compare to those
of other communications technology: computers, CDs, movies?

passing thoughts

One Sunday, before church began, a six-year-old Sunday school student was telling me that he had been watching TV before they had come to church. I teasingly said to him, "You know, Evan, TV will rot your **b r a i n** ." He sighed and said, "I know. And it's bad for my **s o u l** , too."   —*Carol Loeppky*

We don't have a TV but I've tried to help our children avoid the **g o o d / e v i l** dichotomies that children (and many adults) are so apt to make especially if parents have strong values. I didn't know that my attempts had paid off, though, until Nathan was in grade two. The mother of Nathan's friend told me what Nathan had said at their house. The TV was on in their home, and the mother suddenly recalled that we didn't have a TV. She asked Nathan if he was allowed to watch TV. He said, "We're not against watching TV. It's just not the **f o c u s** of our lives."   —*Sue Klassen*

Our children are twelve, ten, eight and six. We try to limit television watching as much as possible. The kids don't watch TV during the school week, and generally watch public TV when they do watch. It definitely limits the **t e m p t a t i o n** to want things! We also try to watch videos that are in line with our values, or what we deem appropriate.   —*Bonnie Ward*

We have never had more than one television in our house and we've always tried to keep it in a **n o n - p r o m i n e n t** place. When we lived in an old house with only one living area (no family room or basement), we bought an enclosed cabinet in which to keep the television. Thus when it wasn't being used, it was out of sight.   —*Joetta Handrich Schlabach*

Our daughter Anna, who is almost six, does not seem to feel that she is missing out on something because we don't watch TV. Since we do not own a VCR, occasionally we take a video to her grandparents' or a friend's home and watch it there. This way it becomes an **o p p o r t u n i t y** to visit someone as well.
                                                          —*Sue Getman*

We do not have a TV or VCR. Next to teaching God's principles from the Bible, this is the most effective thing we've done to influence our children to live **c o n t e n t e d** lives. Here are some of the benefits: When our children (age 7, 5, 4) get asked by others, "What do you want for your birthday?" they usually get a blank look on their faces, **c r i n k l e** their noses, and begin thinking and thinking. They have a hard time coming up with anything. When our children pretend, they **p r e t e n d** Robinson Crusoe, Treasure Island, and Little House on the Prairie, not Power Rangers and Pokemon.   —*April Pekary*

Television: it goes into a box for **s u m m e r**. Our northern prairie summers are too short to spend time in front of the TV.   —*Margaret Rempel*

Our family **" f a s t s "** from TV and movies on Sundays.   —*Ted Lewis*

My friend Nichole says, "Why don't you have a big screen TV?" Because we have an old-fashioned TV and sometimes I do mind it. But sometimes I don't because then you aren't **s i t t i n g** in front of a TV twenty-four hours a day.

—*Alison, age 11*

try this

pretend you are from Mars. Watch TV through the eyes of an outsider and try to figure out what this culture values and what people are like.[3]

lay down the reasons instead of laying down the law. Make sure children understand why you make choices to have no TV, to watch only certain programs or on certain days, to put the TV in an out-of-the-way location.

mute the commercials when your family watches TV. Explain to children how advertising promotes consumption.

use educational TV. Watch it together with children, talk about it, use ideas from it for creative activities away from TV.

make tv size fit your values. Big screen, tiny, or something in between may affect how much your family watches television. Think about it if you buy a new TV.

break down advertisements. Watch TV ads with children and discuss them. What is effective or creative? How do ads sell a lifestyle to promote a product? Work with children to make up your own ads for values you support.

use the pause button. Stop the VCR to talk about questions children may have or things you want to discuss.

count the hours. Make sure children have enough time for play and other activities other than television. Have regular hours of the day or week when TV is or is not allowed.

discuss what you watch. Children will see inappropriate things on TV at times; give them tools to deal with it. Help young children understand they can stop watching if a show at a friend's house is frightening. Talk about attitudes, behaviors, and stereotypes you find offensive on TV programs, so that children are aware of this when they watch TV.

avoid the good/evil split— remember that forbidden fruit is sweeter. If you are honest about both the good and bad sides of television viewing, children are more likely to learn to accept limitations and think critically about TV.

fast from TV and movies on Sundays. Or try a week without television, then have a family discussion about what you liked and didn't like about doing without TV.

put the TV where you want it. Location affects use; think about the effects of putting the TV in the living room, in a child's room, in a basement or side room, in a closed cupboard.

do your homework. Make sure you know what TV programs and movies are about and their rating before you give permission to view.

9.

responding to school commercialism

Encourage children to identify themselves as creators
rather than consumers.

"Pour out your heart like water before the presence of the Lord!
Lift your hands to him for the lives of your children."
                         —*Lamentations 2:19, NRSV*

"Teach [children] to choose the right path,
and when [they are] older
[they] will
remain upon it."
                         MEDITATION **neat prizes, guilt, and food pyramids**
                         —*Proverbs 22:6,*
                         Living Bible

When my children were five years old they started kindergarten. Within three weeks they came home with papers asking them to sell candy, greeting cards, gift wrap, and cheese to neighbors, friends, and relatives. My first reaction was to look through the catalog and see what was available. My second reaction was, "Wow, these things are expensive!" I quickly realized that I did not need anything in the catalog and did not feel comfortable having my two young children, accompanied by me, out selling the items that I felt benefitted the companies more than the school. Nor did I feel it was a worthwhile use of my time.

I was bothered by the push for consumerism, buying and selling unneeded, overpriced goods. When I talked to friends from church they, too, were concerned about the messages sent by the schools to our children. There are several parts to this message. First they get the kids pumped and excited to sell during an assembly, where all the big and little prizes are demonstrated. My children come home saying, "I want to get the neat prizes and the great bike!" This pushes the consumer mentality and helps distinguish the rich from the poor. Some families and relatives can afford to buy these items. Others are barely able to afford school supplies.

The second message from school is that children should use the "guilt mentality" to make a sale. If young children ask you to buy candy or cookies from them, a feeling of guilt or not being generous arises and fuels their goal of selling more merchandise. Children quickly pick up on this "guilt mentality" that is directed at them by adults and corporations. I have heard some children say, "You're too poor (or stingy, or mean, or . . .) to buy me the toy." The "guilt" is hard to overcome.

The third message is to buy, buy, buy. Schoolchildren see these messages everywhere in subtle, but persistent ways. The poster of the food pyramid is sponsored by a major food corporation that illustrates its foods in the pyramid. A breakfast cereal maker "gives away $5,000" to the school that can get the most parents and children to come to a breakfast of their prepackaged sugared cereal, milk, and spoon. The same cereal company gave each child coupons and a coloring book about eating a nutritional breakfast of their brand of cereal. The other side of the school lunch menu is sponsored by the Dairy Council with many tidbits of how to eat more dairy foods. This persistent advertising to a huge captive audience benefits the corporation and undermines the nutritional information being given in the school.

I realize that the school needs support and my children are going to this school. I talk to my children about my concerns. God wants us to be generous and good stewards of our money. We decide to make a donation in the amount that the children can get the minimum prize. This way the school gets all the money, my children get one prize, and we are being generous with our God-given resources.

I also have decided that the school needs my support in other ways. God wants me to be a good steward of my time and help others. I can volunteer to be on the fundraising committee and bring up some of my concerns. I can volunteer in my child's classroom and assist the teachers in whatever they need help with. I can write and call the principal and express my concerns about the mixed messages being given to the children about nutrition while promoting expensive sugared cereals. I can explain the effects of poor nutrition on the learning of children in the school.

I can go further and work with the school to get an organic garden going on school grounds. Each child gets a chance to work in the garden and see how things grow, the school cafeteria gets fresh produce, and the school raises money and awareness by selling the extra produce to the community.

—*Marie Harnish*

the school setting can encourage commercialism in subtle ways. Children may be asked to write letters to Santa detailing their many wants. Math worksheets may ask students to figure out how many items can be purchased with a given amount of money—without giving students the option of spending less money than they hypothetically have on hand. "Show and Tell" may turn into a toy competition. Students compare the individually packaged contents of their character lunch boxes in the cafeteria. Getting dressed in the morning can become time consuming as the "right" clothing is selected.

The school can also choose to deliberately invite commercial messages directed to the children. Many schools, faced with inadequate funding, turn to corporations for "free" learning materials or advertising agreements that will bring revenues into the schools.

Commercialism also confronts our children in school through contests, incentives and samples. Some school districts make exclusive agreements with soft drink manufacturers to have a monopoly on product sales on the school grounds. The schools are offered monetary incentives if a certain amount of the soft drink is consumed by the students on the school grounds. Schools place vending machines strategically and allow kids to drink soft drinks all day long.[1]

"Educational" programs and materials which prominently feature a corporation's name or logo are marketing and not philanthropy. "A business' first responsibility is to the people who own it. That usually means making the largest profit as quickly as possible. In contrast, public schools belong to us all, and exist to promote the public welfare . . . by educating a literate citizenry, capable of think-

how are corporations involved in my local school system?

ing critically and contributing to a democratic society."[2]

When schools allow corporations to target children, education suffers. Advertising's goal is to persuade. Education aims to get children to step back and critically question the messages they hear and the sources of those messages. "We have to teach our children to be media literate. . . . For example, children should be taught about how advertising influences them so they are better able to deal with it, and they need to know as soon as possible. We should ask our schools to develop curricula to teach media literacy, and support them in their attempts."[3] Can schools teach media literacy while at the same time selling students' attention and class time to advertisers?

We can help our children to value critical thinking by limiting the influence of corporations in our schools. The National PTA Principles for Corporate Involvement in the Schools state, "Corporate involvement shall not require students to observe, listen to, or read commercial advertising." This is not the reality in most schools. The principles also state that "selling or providing access to a captive audience in the classroom for commercial purposes is exploitation and a violation of the public trust."[4]

The Consumer's Union, the nonprofit publisher of *Consumer Reports* Magazine, offers these suggestions for parents:

—*Support the idea that schools should be ad-free zones, where young people can pursue learning free from commercial influences and pressures.*

—*Support the adoption of guidelines developed by the International Organization of Consumers Unions, which call for all business-sponsored educational materials to be accurate, objective, complete, nondiscriminatory, noncom-*

how do I deal with tensions between home messages and school messages?

how do I become aware of school messages of commercialism?

mercial, and evaluative.

—*Teach children to evaluate commercial content in all the materials they receive, including those in the schools. Regularly discuss purchasing and money management decisions with children, and analyze advertising with them.*

—*Address the larger problem of underfunding of our schools.*[5]

how does my faith inform my response to commercial messages in the school?

what noncommercial means could improve the quality of education at my local school?

how might I be an advocate for my children or other children in local schools?

passing thoughts

We don't like making people feel **obligated** to buy something just because it's a child selling the items. We ask grandparents and an aunt and uncle once, but we do not insist they make a purchase. Often the fundraising offers the incentive of prizes for the greatest amount sold. We choose to allow our child an evening of activity of her **choice**, or a special meal request. Our daughter seems to understand and accept that she will not be the high seller of the fundraiser.   —*Darlene Schmidt*

I find fundraisers at school, and elsewhere, **frustrating**. We participate as a rule, unless it's poor value or just junk. Then we give a donation in lieu and we were even instrumental in getting our kids' school to "count" donations as **participation** in fundraising for the purposes of the competitions they seem always to hold. We discuss the whole thing with our kids and sometimes go through the catalog with them and explain why we aren't buying things. For example, wrapping paper. We explain that we prefer to use reusable bags, because they are environmentally less wasteful and cheaper in the long term. The kids don't seem to have any trouble with this.   —*Michelle Bull*

I was unhappy last year when Kellogg's was having a contest and the winner would get $5,000 if that school had the most parents coming in for a **prepackaged** Kellogg's breakfast with sugared cereal and milk. I was very upset and talked to the principal about my concerns, talked to the children about why I talked to her, and **b o y c o t t e d** the breakfast. The children understood the reasons. If Channel One comes to the school, I will protest loudly. (Channel One News is a daily, televised, 10-minute, newscast beamed via satellite during the school year to each of the 12,000 American middle, junior, and high schools in the Channel One Network community. It includes advertisements targeted at students.)

—Marie Harnish

Ideas for **n o n c o m m e r c i a l** fundraisers:

—A **f u n** fair or festival with snacks and prizes donated by local merchants
—A used winter clothing and equipment sale (includes mittens, snowsuits, boots, sleds, skis, ski boots, skates, shovels, hockey equipment, and snowblowers)
—A school-wide garage sale
—A used book sale
—A silent **a u c t i o n**
—A community dinner
—A bottle and can collection in places where there is a deposit on containers
—A work-for-pay day
—A film night
—A donated **m u s i c a l** performance
—Selling a nutritious, edible product   *—Jeanne Zimmerly Jantzi*

try this

support schools in nonfinancial ways: volunteer, assist teachers, and suggest less commercial fundraising options.

make a direct donation when children solicit for schools, instead of buying the overpriced candy bars and wrapping paper.

teach children to evaluate commercial content in all the materials they receive. Analyze advertising with them. Teach them to think critically and ask questions about commercialism in school.

encourage ties between local businesses and schools, so that schools have less need for corporate sponsorship.

speak your mind. If you are concerned about Channel One, product placement, or advertising in schools, let school officials know.

10.

choosing playthings

Participate in children's lives by providing opportunities
for creative play.

*But speaking the truth in love, we must grow up in every way into him who is the head,
into Christ, from whom the whole body, joined and knit together by every ligament
with which it is equipped, as each part is working properly,
promotes the body's growth
in building itself up
in love.*
—*Ephesians 4:15-16, NRSV*

MEDITATION **discovering everyday adventures**

Surely one of the joys of parenting is watching your child happily at play. Not always, but often, the play involves a plaything, whether it be an expensive brand-name toy or a common cardboard box. Exploring how things feel, and move, and work, is part of the wonderful process of growth and discovery. For children, play is important work; playthings are their tools.

The biblical witness enjoins followers of Christ to grow up in every way into Christ, and our current wisdom recognizes that we do grow in many different ways. Ideally, our physical selves, social selves, intellectual selves and spiritual selves will be encouraged to grow every day. Will that growth be in the direction of Christ? Will the child's playthings help or hinder?

Parents of faith want to make thoughtful choices about the playthings that become part of their child's world. What tools do we wish to equip our children with as they dig, pour, ride, slide, imagine, experiment, acquire and share their way through their day?

Marvelous playthings may be created out of yogurt containers, Popsicle sticks, tape, pinecones, and like treasures. We have designated a cupboard as our craft area and keep it stocked with recycled supplies and found objects. A simple reminder to visit the craft area usually takes care of an "I don't know what to do" complaint.

This kind of play has its hazards: creative projects are often messy projects! Without careful negotiations, science experiments can soon crowd the cook out of the kitchen. When children are small, ordinary household tasks can become great adventures. They may take longer to complete, but what better way to learn?

Building blocks, sandbox, Legos, little animals, markers (and more markers), books (and more books), puppets, puzzles, rhythm instruments, Play-doh, dress-up clothes, bicycles, and collectibles (fossils, coins, etc.) are all examples of play-things our boys have enjoyed that we feel help them grow in wholesome ways.

There are also difficult decisions to be made. We have some computer games but monitor time spent in front of the screen. Many days it is difficult to stick to the agreed-upon limits. We do not allow pretend guns at our house. Period. When some come out at the neighbors' house on occasion, we are not pleased, but have decided not to interfere. When the boys come home, however, they know we will have a chat (again!) about why we do not have guns at our house.

What we do have at our house right now is an interest in clubs. A sign at our front door proclaims, The Amazing Adventure Club. Perhaps I should move this sign to our church door! Hung there it may remind us, thanks to our children, that every day can be an adventure as we seek to grow up in every way into Christ.

As our children's bodies grow taller and stronger, hopefully their hearts, and souls, and minds will too. How will yours bounce, cut, cuddle, roll, or bang their way toward God today?

—Ann Weber Becker

A
CLOSER
LOOK

Jesus reminded his disciples that "one's life does not consist in the abundance of possessions" (Luke 12:15). Neither does children's creative development or happiness consist in an abundance of toys on a shelf. A child's abundant life includes opportunities for creative play and opportunities to play with other children.

Playing with others gives children the chance to become aware of others' feelings and to learn the give-and-take necessary for cooperation. Children playing together spark a sort of creative energy as one idea builds on another and playthings are created or used in new ways. I have often watched it happen. A friend comes to visit, appraises the available play materials, and soon new play activities are invented.

Playthings that promote creativity and cooperative play may be purchased, made with loving hands, or discovered. Not all playthings must be found in the toy box.

Good playthings are not always labeled as toys. Quality playthings can be anything that children have permission to use in their creative endeavors. One way to develop the play possibilities of your home is to consider the creative areas around the house and set boundaries for their use.

Our kitchen sometimes becomes a creative laboratory.

The bathtub provides a different play experience. Old toys can be used in new ways by bringing them to the water.

The closet is a costume wardrobe for dramatic play. Dress-up clothes stretch the imagination as children deck themselves with shoes, clothes and accessories.

what toys in my home sit forgotten on the shelves? why are they seldom used?

My sewing area suggests creative projects when materials are accessible and available. We keep a big box of fabric scraps for project purposes.

At the workbench real things become play materials. Our children learned which tools they could use on their own and which tools require adult supervision.

Versatile toys are open-ended. Their shape can change or they can be used in many ways. Building toys such as wooden blocks, Legos or K'nex can be used to create endless varieties of toys. Clay, paper, dolls, vehicles, dress-up clothes, and animal figures are also versatile and open-ended.

Quality toys are durable. Wooden toys, cloth toys, and washable, heavy duty plastic toys will survive the years.

Good toys encourage cooperative play. Contributor Bonnie Ward calls this "shareability." For example, I can measure the low shareability of my sons' Game Boy by how often conflicts arise over its use. Only one person at a time can play it, and while they play, they tune out everyone else. If a toy is shareable, it offers an even more satisfying play experience when more than one person plays with it. A basket of building toys, a long jump rope, a homemade puppet theater, or a sled with room for two rate high for encouraging cooperative play.

Playthings are a major focal point in the life of a child. As parents of faith, our choices of playthings can encourage our children to develop the capacity for creativity and cooperation.

what playthings in my home do I feel good about?   what playthings bother me?

what connections do I see between playthings and faith?

what were some of my favorite playthings as a child? what made them so good?

passing thoughts

Riding **bicycle** has been perhaps our son Isaac's overall favorite activity since we moved to Irian Jaya, Indonesia. Sometimes, when Isaac wished he had a motorcycle instead of a plain old bicycle, he slipped a flattened plastic water bottle under the bike frame so that it rubbed against the knobby back tire with a roaring sound, an **ingenious** technique he picked up from our Irianese neighbor kids.   —*Laura Lindell*

We spend most of our toy money on Duplos, Legos, blocks, Playmobil, etc.—toys that have multiple uses and encourage group play. When our kids want "junk" or fad toys, we encourage them to **consider** the value and quality and talk about need. If they still are set on something, we make them use their own money or wait until a birthday or Christmas. Often **waiting** decreases the interest!   —*Bonnie Ward*

I try to be creative with things around the house—Lydia carries a basket of **clothespins** around, and enjoys dumping them and picking them up. She digs in the dirt with an old spoon and a yogurt container, instead of a plastic kid's shovel and bucket.   —*Winnie Brubaker Haggard*

create a craft corner. Have a place in the house where markers, paints, paper, cardboard, glue, etc., is available for creative projects.

try this

make playthings out of found objects: yogurt containers, pinecones, sticks, clothespins, rubber bands.

use leftover materials: give children old clothes, fabric scraps, plastic pipe, or wood scraps from a project.

do science experiments in the kitchen. Make volcanoes with vinegar and baking soda. Find new uses for funnels, cookie cutters, and lids. Supervise children's creation of their own snack concoctions.

think about creative potential when buying toys. Will a toy have one use or many? Is it a one-child toy or can more children use it at once?

limit advertising directed at children when possible. Talk about ads when faced with them; how accurate are they, how long would the toy last, how does it compare to toys that have remained favorites?

shift locations to give old toys a new life. Move kitchen items to the bathtub, indoor toys to the outdoors, dress-up clothes or games to the attic.

factor in grandparents and relatives. Buy fewer toys for children at holidays if you know many toys will come from extended family as gifts.

throw out ideas to encourage cooperative play: Start a club, invent a game, and build a cardboard house. Make your home a welcoming place for other children.

make decisions about controversial toys. For example, are toy guns forbidden at home? At friends' houses? Okay for hunting but not for shooting people? If there are toys you don't like but are willing to let your children use, talk with them about your views.

start playing! Be available to spend time playing with children, giving ideas, and being an audience.

suggest real things for playthings: flashlights, backpacks, a scarf, blankets, and binoculars. Suggest scenarios: Maybe you're going camping, you're explorers, you're snowbound in winter.

11.

creating family traditions

Practice family customs that pass along our values.

He was praying in a certain place, and after he had finished, one of his disciples said to him,
      "Lord, teach us to pray, as John taught his disciples."
   He said to them, "When you pray, say: Father, hallowed be your name. Your kingdom come.
Give us each day our daily bread. And forgive us our sins, for we ourselves
forgive everyone indebted to us.
      And do not bring us to the time of trial."
      —Luke 11:1-4, NRSV

MEDITATION **in unison around the table**

When I was a kid we always said the same table grace, "Come, Lord Jesus, be our guest. Let these gifts to us be blessed. Amen." It was a perfunctory ritual.

Rituals are important. Table grace is important! But from my childhood experience I have vowed not to say the same table grace twice in a row, and to share the honor of saying it with others. Sometimes there's a nice quiet time before the Spirit moves someone to pray. Then sometimes the prayer is long, sometimes it's short. Sometimes it's deep, sometimes it's funny. We've sung the Johnny Appleseed song. We've even sung "Praise God from Whom All Blessings Flow" to the tune of "Hernando's Hideaway."

I had a "dry period" in my spiritual life when I wasn't sure if prayer was anything more than talking to myself, a form of self-therapy. During that time our son was quite young. One day I realized that I'd never taught him the Lord's Prayer. So I began praying with him at night. That helped me to come alive spiritually again.

Years later when Peter was twenty, he gave me one of the best Christmas gifts I have ever received—a hand-made, framed certificate of thanks for the major things I had given him. Yep, there it was in print . . . thanks for teaching him how to pray.

When we pray together in unison, our favorite is a variation of my childhood prayer, "Come, Lord Jesus." The very important second verse is "Blessed be God who is our bread. May all the world be clothed and fed."

Our mealtime prayers are rarely "complete" prayers. They usually focus on thanks. It's helpful for us all to know the components of prayer. I learned the acronym ACTS. "A" is to acknowledge God as the one to whom we are praying, the one we hold dear and worthy, the one who can and will hear our prayers. "C" is to confess our sins. "T" is to thank God for life and all blessings, including the forgiveness of our sins. "S" is supplications or "askings."

The posture of prayer—folding hands, kneeling, etc.—is important. When praying by myself I open my hands and turn the cupped palms toward heaven symbolizing that I am open to whatever God has for me.

We always hold hands at the table to say grace. The communal relationship at mealtime is primary. Nothing must interfere with the family or household eating at least one meal together each day.

—Gerald Iversen

A
CLOSER
LOOK

When this book was in its planning stages I met with a group of young people in Philadelphia who ranged in age from eleven to thirteen. When I asked them about their families' special traditions, most leaned forward to enthusiastically join the conversation. With pride they detailed the unique ways their families did things. These customs formed consistent patterns repeated over and over in their lives. The family "ways of doing things" had become part of these young people's identities.

Anyone who stays as a guest in another's home soon realizes the host family's unique ways of doing even the ordinary things—from bedtime routines, to meal-time prayers, to the way of opening Christmas gifts. Family traditions form around our common practices—the kind of vacations our family typically takes or our usual ways of spending time together. Still other traditions are rituals: lighting the Advent candles or saying "I love you" each morning as a child goes off to school.

As people of faith, our family traditions underscore what we value. We may light the Advent candles to enter into our faith story. We may choose to spend vacations outdoors because we stand in awe and wonder at what God has created. We may set aside regular and special times together because we value each other. We join with others in the broader family of faith as we celebrate Easter. We focus on God's provision for us and our connections to others when we ask God's blessing on our meals.

As parents, we can create family customs that show we value each other and the time we spend together. These family traditions or routines can make children

is our household able to have a meal together every day?
if not, what can we change to make that happen?

feel a loving sense of structure and order in their lives.

At age nineteen, Ron Fox described his family's rediscovered custom:

Sharing a family meal wasn't something that happened a lot around my house. The daily dinnertime routine when I was growing up in Richmond was to come home and find no one around but me.

Now, after five years of living apart, I'm spending my senior year of high school living in Gary, Indiana, with my father and sister. The thing I value most is the supper we share. Every night all of us . . . sit down to dinner together. . . . We trade off cooking different nights. If someone can't be there, we save him some food. We look out for each other like that.

Maybe this doesn't sound like such a big deal, but it's something I've never experienced before. . . . For a long time I pretended to myself that I didn't care whether I ate alone. Now I know how good it feels to sit down every night and share a meal with my family. It means we're taking care of each other.[1]

Many contributors for this resource wrote about spending holiday time visiting friends or extended family or going camping. Visiting people emphasizes the value of relationships and connections with others. Outdoor holidays connect us to our Creator.

Camping is almost a modern synonym for sojourning. It gives us a chance to grow deeply attached to a place for a few hours, days, or weeks knowing that we will leave it, but cherishing it all the more for that. For many people, camping in unspoiled creation awakens for the first time an awareness both of what God has given us and how we often misuse it.[2]

As parents, we can also create family customs around praying together at

which family traditions are full of meaning for me? for children in my family or extended family? which traditions could become more meaningful?

mealtimes. When we do this, we not only connect with other family members, but also with the larger faith community. As we ask God's blessing on our food, we focus on our dependence on God's provision and express our thanks to God. Contributor Becky T. Nickel wrote about her family's way of focusing to pray.

We arrive at the dinner table in a huff . . . high energy, low patience, no focus on receiving the food as gifts from God. I've found that taking three or four deep breaths helps all of us settle in for a mealtime. I usually do the counting aloud as we deep breathe.

When families develop traditions for spending time together, praying together, or taking holidays together they help children know a secure place in the world. Parents and children have the opportunity to share their faith in concrete ways. "Ways of doing things," reflected through all aspects of family life, reveal the core of who we are, what we believe, and what we value.

in what ways do my family's holidays or vacations reflect our faith?

what childhood traditions have I maintained and what have I changed with my own children?

does my church have regular traditions with children?

are there family rituals that can be adapted for church settings?

church rituals that can be adapted for families?

passing thoughts

We have started a tradition that our kids really enjoy, called "Pioneer Night." On those **n i g h t s** we use kerosene lamps, candles, the fireplace, etc. We talk about living in the olden days, take baths by **c a n d l e l i g h t**, play games together, read stories, etc. The kids really enjoy the mood set by not using electricity, and it reminds us of what we really love.   —*Bonnie Ward*

There are days when "simple, joyful, and generous" do not seem to be part of our vocabulary. For years we've had a banner in our dining room: "Attitude is the mind's **p a i n t b r u s h**. It can color any situation." Then there is another: "Cooperation is better than conflict." Between these two and a third— about taking the risks of peace instead of war—we have a backdrop for the **j o y s** and conflicts of our lives around a common table. We have made one meal a day **t o g e t h e r** family time over the years. We do different things (besides eat) around the table: read chapter books, memorize a Scripture verse or passage, take turns telling about our day.   —*Mary Ann Conrad*

When the children were young, our nighttime **r i t u a l** was to say to them, "I am with you," and they would respond "and will keep you in all places." "I will trust," we would say, and they said, "and not be afraid." I will both lie down and sleep in peace; for you alone, O Lord, make me lie down in safety.
          —*Naomi Lederach*

We make **s p e c i a l** dinners occasions for celebration. When my husband began working in the corporate world, we celebrated a raise or recognition with a pizza, the only time we bought a ready-to-eat pizza. Over time, that celebration has grown to include anyone's **a c h i e v e m e n t s**. When our children are accepted into the college of their choice, get a job, or get an award, they **t r e a t** the family to their choice of a meal, either at home or in a restaurant.

—*Linda Price*

Now that both children read well, on weekends we sometimes have a reading time together. Each person curls up in a **c o m f o r t a b l e** chair or sofa in the family room with a book they are reading. We read silently together. It's a **s o o t h i n g** time; it's quiet (no radio or music) and relaxing. We're also together and even though we're not talking we feel each other's presence. We all love this time together.   —*Kelli Burkholder King*

One of our favorite family activities is the extended family vacation we take every year with **a u n t s**, uncles, grandparents, and cousins. We each bring food and groceries. We share the cooking; two people cook each evening for the whole group. Days are free to do activities together or apart as we desire. From supper time through the evening we are all together. Over the years we have developed a variety of rituals that are free and fun. We have a music night when everyone plays an instrument, their voice, or one they **i n v e n t**. One person used grass for her instrument one year. One night, usually toward the end of the week, we have poetry night.   —*Marie Harnish*

Times that we spend together as a family usually include outdoor fun: walking out in the country, picnicking, swimming, **s k a t i n g** , cross-country skiing, or throwing ourselves into snowbanks. We usually cycle to our destinations, weather and practicality permitting, but commonly the question arises, "Do we have to ride our bikes?" How do we keep this practice **j o y f u l** for all, as it truly is for us old parents?   —*Brenda MacDonald*

We frequently used the following **c o v e n a n t** prayer for evening devotionals when our three children were growing up. We'd sit on the floor in the living room for sharing, Bible reading, and prayers. It became meaningful to all of us. I don't know who wrote it, but it was long ago.

God made us a family   We need each other
                    We love one another
            We forgive one another
        We work **t o g e t h e r**
    We play together
We worship together   Together we use God's word
                    Together we **g r o w** in Christ
            Together we love all people
        Together we serve our God
    Together we hope for heaven
These are our **h o p e s** and ideals
    Help us to attain them, O God,
            Through Jesus Christ our Lord.   —*Cornelius J. and Wilma L. Dyck*

try this

create a bedtime ritual. Sing a song, rock together, tell a story, and say a Bible verse or reassuring prayer together.

have a picnic. Getting a blanket, making sandwiches together, and heading for the backyard makes lunchtime special for young children.

take a family day together. Leave the normal routine and work life and have an outing or special activity.

create a pioneer night with children. Use only kerosene lamps and candles, play games, read stories, and talk about life before modern technology.

try a new table grace before meals. Get ideas from songbooks, devotionals, and hymnbooks. Try a silent grace or spontaneous prayers from family members. Hold hands together as a family when saying grace.

take a walk or bike ride together, with plenty of time to relax and talk.

take turns naming something each person is thankful for at table or bedtime prayers.

share a meal together. Decide how often your family wants to eat together and stick to it. If you have full schedules write it in so that it really happens.

teach the Lord's Prayer to children. Use it as a table grace or bedtime prayer.

spend time around the table. Not only meals, but times for reading books to children, telling each other about the day, memorizing Scripture verses.

go on an extended family vacation with grandparents, aunts, uncles, cousins. Do inexpensive things like camping so that no one is left out due to cost. Keep the agenda simple and open, leave free time, share cooking responsibility. Spend evenings together talking, singing, or doing whatever you enjoy.

light advent candles as a family during the Christmas season.

read together. Set aside a regular reading time with no TV, radio, or music.

try church rituals in your home. Light a candle, read a Bible verse for the day or week, and make a banner that reflects the season or upcoming holiday.

make up your own sung prayer. Put a Bible verse to a simple tune. Or sing the first verse of a well-known hymn for a prayer.

tell a story. Draw on your own storehouse of memories and stories: from your childhood, your parents' childhood, fables, and Bible stories, etc.

cook a special dinner at home or eat out to celebrate milestones: school awards, job promotions, and goals reached.

play outdoors together. Go for hikes or go camping. Take along the Psalms for reading about God's creation, and nature guides for learning about it.

12.

celebrating together

Give special attention to why and how we celebrate.

One generation shall laud your works to another. . . .
On the glorious splendor of your majesty,
             and on your wondrous works,
    I will meditate. . . .
They shall celebrate the fame of your abundant goodness. . . .
—Psalm 145:4-7, NRSV

MEDITATION **overwhelmed with wonder**

after church one Sunday in the fall, our friend Brenda invites us to join her family for her birthday picnic on the banks of the South Saskatchewan River. The Canada geese and sandhill cranes are migrating, and Brenda and Wayne know of a place along the river valley where the geese and cranes stop for food and water. We jump at the opportunity to join these dear friends for what we know will be an excellent adventure.

Later in the afternoon, cars filled with blankets, coolers, and adventurers, we follow the river south of the city, traveling down a highway, then a gravel road, then a dirt trail through a field, until we stop at the edge of the prairie river valley. The nine of us, ages four to forty-something, clamber down the riverbank to explore the sandbars on the river. The intricately patterned windswept sand gives way to footprints and names etched with sticks.

Back on the bank overlooking the wide river valley, we

unfold blankets over the prairie grasses and set out our breads, cheeses, and garden vegetables. As the sun lowers itself into the western sky, we warm our bodies with hot chocolate and coffee. And as the cool autumn air entices us into warmer jackets, mittens, and toques, the sky begins to beckon.

Seeking food and shelter they come. Small flocks at first. Geese and sandhill cranes, honking and garbling their way toward the river. Then, as the sky turns to dusk, the flocks become larger and more frequent. The cranes make magnificently clumsy landings on the water, then stand side by side around the edges of the sandbars. We huddle on the sheltered riverbank, binoculars focused on the birds, skies, and water. Look over there, and there, and over here. Awesome. Amazing. "How do they know to come here?" asks a child. We sit there, leaning against the earth, with dear friends around us, spellbound by the natural pattern of things. Happy birthday, Brenda.

I've pondered this event many times in the months that have followed. I am the party person at our house. That is, I usually plan for and orchestrate the party times—birthdays, Christmas, Easter, and holidays. Often I overwhelm myself with details, excess, and convoluted preparations, all in an attempt to provide heart-warming memorable events. Brenda's riverbank birthday was so refreshing and memorable, because we simply enjoyed our place on the earth, overwhelmed not with planning details but with the wonder of the seasonal world.

My daughter says, "Mom, do you remember when we went to the river with Wayne and Brenda to see the cranes? Mom, can we do it again?" Through our celebrations, can we see ourselves as part of something larger? A sacred moment? A community of friends? A seasonal rhythm of nature?

—*Eileen Klassen Hamm*

A
CLOSER
LOOK

Celebrations mark a joyful break from the ordinary. We share our gladness with others who set aside their routines to celebrate something special. Celebrations underscore and emphasize what is important to us; yet sometimes the preparations and hoopla make us lose sight of exactly what and why we celebrate.

When Jesus came to visit in her home, Martha became upset about all the work she had to do while her sister Mary sat listening at Jesus' feet. Jesus responded, "Martha, Martha! You are worried and troubled over so many things, but just one is needed. Mary has chosen the right thing, and it will not be taken away from her" (Luke 10:41-42, TEV). Preparing the joyful meal to celebrate Jesus' visit distracted Martha from spending time with the honored guest.

How can we focus on what matters most as we celebrate with children? Christmas, for example, celebrates Immanuel, God with us. Although many of us would say that we value family time at Christmas, we may actually have less relaxed time to enjoy the people with us. How can our celebrating reflect what we believe? Could we "make Christmas a time to be with others—spending our time with God, with friends and family, and with the creation that God made?"[1]

When we focus on what and why we celebrate, our celebrations become more meaningful. Instead of distracting our children, everything we do points toward our reason for celebrating.

The gift giving that often accompanies celebrations such as Christmas or birthdays recalls God's gift to us and allows us to share our lives with others. When we give gifts in all seasons, we remember how much we rely on other people and we

what are my children's favorite celebrations? why?

in what ways do my family's celebrations reflect our faith or interests?

recognize that all we have is a gift.

Celebrations allow parents and children a time for unbridled creativity. Children can participate in creating celebrations meaningful to the whole family. The first step is defining exactly what and why we are celebrating. For birthday celebrations, for example, my own family's purposes are to honor the birthday person, to be with other people, and to have fun.

Marie Harnish describes one of her extended family's celebration traditions during their annual group vacation.

One night, usually toward the end of the week, we have poetry night. This is not your typical poetry, this is the Harnish family creative poetry. Each person starts by writing three lines of poetry about a chosen vacation theme. It could be the beach, or the food, or the house we stay in, or whatever fits that year. The writer then covers all but the last line, and passes the poem to the next person, who writes two more lines, and covers up all but one. In this way we have a hilarious poem that sometimes makes sense, but gets the whole family laughing hysterically! These rituals have helped our children enjoy the family with all its idiosyncrasies.

As people of faith, we want to celebrate in ways that point us toward God and that communicate to our children our love for them.

what influences your celebration expectations or your children's expectations of how occasions should be celebrated?

what could my family change in birthday or holiday celebrations so we could spend more time on the things most meaningful to us?

What holidays besides Christmas can be made more meaningful and less commercial?

passing thoughts

Our decision to host our children's birthday parties at home (rather than the local fast-food place) has been joyful as several guests have proclaimed these "the best party I've ever been to!" What was so great? A backwards, **u p s i d e - d o w n** , inside-out party that included crazy dressing up and a science party creating new instruments out of household junk. Guests simply relished being in our home and ate a well-balanced meal with glee.   —*Susan Mark Landis*

Our children place all the figures of the   **m a n g e r**   scene around the house—the shepherds in a field nearby; the wise kings in different "countries"; and Mary, Joseph, and the donkey **t r a v e l i n g** to Bethlehem. Each night the people move closer to their destination. The baby Jesus arrives on December 25.
—*Marie Harnish*

When we were in Central America we were introduced to the custom of having a late dinner on Christmas Eve and opening gifts after **m i d n i g h t** , when the Christ child arrived and was laid in the manger scene. Our family now attends church on Christmas Eve, returns home to open gifts, and then enjoys a special candlelight dinner **t o g e t h e r** .   —*Joetta Handrich Schlabach*

Each year we set aside   **p h o t o s**   throughout the months, representing special activities and events. Early in December we have a few reprints made if necessary, and fill two pocket albums. That is the gift our three children give to their grandparents every Christmas. It's not a surprise, but it continues to be just as special every year. Our firstborn is now twenty-two years of age. His grandparents have twenty-two little albums, **c a p t u r i n g** chronologically his life and that of his siblings. The grandparents like to look through them in moments when they feel lonely. Twenty-two years of gifts, and they don't take up much physical space, but they occupy a mountain of **l o v e** and an important sense of family place and belonging. Our children have not been buying something they can't afford for grandparents who do not need any "things."

—*Margaret Rempel*

We keep a special "birthday kit" in a cookie tin. In the kit are candles, matches, a "Happy Birthday" sign for the top of the cake, a hanging "Happy Birthday" banner, plastic cling window decorations, and some **b a l l o o n s**. Sometimes we have been away from home on a birthday. The birthday kit makes the day special even if the "cake" is a pile of graham crackers. The kit also helps us host spur-of-the-moment birthday celebrations when we **d i s c o v e r** that a visitor is having a birthday.   —*Jeanne Zimmerly Jantzi*

Now that we are on retirement income and more grandchildren are being added to the family, brand-new gifts for everyone in the family at one time are cost-prohibitive. We decided on **g a r a g e   s a l e** Christmases. Everyone gets several unique items we have found over the summer at garage sales. We enjoy the fun of seeking out just the right gifts for each family member and the recipients are always "surprised."   —*R. McMahon*

Some parents I know have found that it is a **w o n d e r f u l** birthday
ritual for a child to be given both a new right and a new responsibility each year.
For example, the right to cross the street may bring with it the responsibility of
bringing the **m a i l** in. A child may be allowed to stay up later, but assume
the job of taking the garbage out.   —*David Walsh*[2]

We lived far away from grandparents, aunts, and uncles when our children were
small. Some of the best gifts our children received were an add-on series of cassette
tapes with **g r a n d m a** and other family members reading books, singing
or telling **m e m o r i e s** to our children. Our children would often go to
bed with the tapes playing. The tapes were gifts to me, as well. I loved the feeling
of connection as I relaxed in the warm evening air in Congo and listened to my
mother's voice in the other room, chatting comfortably with my children.
                                                    —*Jeanne Zimmerly Jantzi*

Some neighbors from Austria **i n t r o d u c e d** us to the St. Nicholas Day
tradition. So we began a family tradition that on December 6 (St. Nicholas Day)
we would get a family gift (a game or book for all to enjoy) and also do something for someone in need, such as take baked goods and go visit an elderly person
or a **f r i e n d** with mental illness.   —*Joetta Handrich Schlabach*

When our children were growing up, we gave gifts that were necessities, along
with perhaps one game and a few good books. Now, I like to turn to organizations such as SERVV, Heifer Project International, Alternatives, Habitat for

Humanity for gifts. You can make and give **t i c k e t s** that state such things as you will babysit for a certain number of hours or you will take a neighbor shopping.   —*Ruth Clark*

Rather than focus on gifts during the holidays we try to focus on relationships. When my sister asks what Amy would like for a Christmas, I suggest that they do something **t o g e t h e r** . Instead of giving gifts, we take a family trip together to a nearby city.   —*Libby Caes*

For birthday parties, my husband, Ned, makes homemade **p i z z a** and each child gets to put on the ingredients of his or her choice. I make a carrot cake and ice cream for dessert. Whatever the child didn't eat he or she can take home. Last year each child made a **s c u l p t u r e** out of my craft box—bits and pieces of things I collect over the year. They had a great time doing this. I took pictures of them and they took them home. We had a team scavenger hunt outside for natural things.   —*Marie Harnish*

Favorite gifts tend to be from one uncle who probably spends only about $5 on each, but must spend a lot of time picking out the **p e r f e c t** gift. A few years back he gave our daughter a Chinese fan, the kind you can buy in **C h i n a t o w n** for about $1.50, and she was thrilled, and felt very grown up. Gifts need not be expensive, just well chosen.   —*Michelle Bull*

In recent years for Christmas, we have tried to buy only one significant gift for each child—stressing quality, creativity **p o t e n t i a l**, etc. They get many more gifts from extended family, but we try to direct those choices toward books, needed clothing, or other gifts that we can't afford, but value for their creativity potential, shareability and quality.

—*Bonnie Ward*

try this

give time as a gift. Take hours away from Christmas shopping and spend them with children and family doing holiday projects. Give tickets that specify time gifts: babysitting, taking an elderly friend for a drive, or taking a neighbor shopping.

encourage group participation at birthdays. Instead of restaurant parties, choose games where everyone is involved: piñatas, clown parties, and water parties.

invite friends. Think of celebrations your family does without others, then discuss who you might invite to join you.

shift the focus. Encourage activities and stories that reinforce the religious meaning of holidays like Easter and Christmas.

celebrate the seasons. Make an outdoor expedition to see changing leaf color, migrating birds, and new growth. Collect natural mementos: leaves, stones, seashells. Use them to decorate the house or a child's room, or to make a collage or simple sculpture.

give a new right and a new responsibility to a child for a birthday gift.

encourage cassette tape gifts from grandparents and other extended family if they live far away. Relatives might read books, sing, or tell memories on tape.

offer children security with simple traditions: an Advent wreath, reading the Christmas story together, and singing the same songs.

make giving lists instead of wish lists at Christmas. Help children think about what gifts would be appropriate for their family, friends, and relatives.

help the Holy Family travel to Bethlehem during Advent. Put shepherds, kings, family, and animals around the house and let children move them toward their Nativity set destination each night of Advent, for arrival with the baby Jesus on Christmas.

don't let the food eat your time. Choose activities and celebrations where food preparation doesn't become all-consuming and take some people away from the fun. Or get everyone involved in chopping vegetables, making dessert, or preparing sandwiches.

give supplies for project kits as gifts: fabric and notions for a sewing project, plaster of Paris to mold and decorate, and fabric paints to decorate a shirt. Include a note with the gift of your time, then enjoy working on the project with the recipient.

give small photo books as gifts. Set aside photos of children and family during the year to make into gifts for grandparents at Christmas.

connect with others on holidays. Take token gifts of food to neighbors on Christmas or Easter. Invite people you don't know well or those new to the community for Thanksgiving dinner.

make a birthday pizza. Let each person add the ingredient of his or her choice.

keep a birthday kit with candles, matches, birthday banner, and balloons. Use it for at-home birthdays, when traveling, or for spur-of-the-moment celebrations of a visitor's birthday.

learn new holiday customs and rituals from friends and neighbors, international students, and visitors. Incorporate those that you like into your family's celebrations.

NOTES

CHAPTER 1 **sharing faith**

1   Richard Foster, *Freedom of Simplicity* (San Francisco: Harper & Row, 1981).

CHAPTER 2 **building self-esteem**

1   Victor H. Nelson, "Hospitable Families," *In Context,* #21, Spring 1989. Available at <www.context.org/ICLIB/IC21/Nelson.htm>.
2   *Hymnal: A Worship Book* (Elgin, Illinois: Brethren Press, Newton, Kansas: Faith & Life Press, Scottdale, Pennsylvania: Mennonite Publishing House, 1992).
3   Cecile Andrews, "Building Community," in *Simpler Living Compassionate Life,* ed. Michael Schut (Denver: Earth Ministry, 1999).

CHAPTER 3 **connecting with others**

1   Robert R. Gottfried, *Economics, Ecology, and the Roots of Western Faith* (Lanham, Maryland: Rowman and Littlefield Publishers, Inc., 1995).
2   David Walsh, *Selling Out America's Children* (Minneapolis: Fairview Press, 1994).
3   Andrews.

CHAPTER 4 **spending time**

1 Gerald May, "Entering the Emptiness," in *Simpler Living Compassionate Life*, ed. Michael Schut (Denver: Earth Ministry, 1999).
2 Ibid.
3 Janet Luhrs, *The Simple Living Guide* (New York: Broadway Books, 1997).
4 Ibid.

CHAPTER 5 **caring for creation**

1 Joetta Handrich Schlabach, *Extending the Table* (Scottdale, Pennsylvania: Herald Press, 1991).
2 Gottfried, *Economics, Ecology, and Roots.*
3 Ibid.
4 Ibid.
5 Kathleen McGinnis and James McGinnis, *Parenting for Peace and Justice: Ten Years Later* (Maryknoll, New York: Orbis Books, 1995).
6 Loren Wilkinson and Mary Ruth Wilkinson, *Caring for Creation in Your Own Backyard* (Ann Arbor, Michigan: Servant Publications, 1992).
7 Ibid.

CHAPTER 6 **managing money**

1 Walsh, *Selling Out.*
2 Mark Vincent, *A Christian View of Money* (Scottdale, Pennsylvania: Herald Press, 1997).
3 Joe Dominguez and Vicki Robin, *Your Money or Your Life* (New York: Penguin Books, 1992).
4 Ibid.
5 McGinnis, *Parenting for Peace.*
6 Mennonite Media, "Beyond the News: Money" (Harrisonburg, Virginia: Mennonite Media Productions, 1997).

CHAPTER 7 **shopping**

1 Dominguez and Robin, *Your Money or Your Life.*
2 Walsh, *Selling Out.*
3 Alan Durning, "How Much Is Enough?" in *Simpler Living Compassionate Life*, ed. Michael Schut (Denver: Earth Ministry, 1999).
4 Tom Atlee, "The Conversion of the American Dream," in *In Context*, #26, Summer 1990. Available at <www.context.org/ICLIB/IC26/Atlee.htm>.

CHAPTER 8 **deciding about television**

1 Walsh, *Selling Out.*
2 Ibid.
3 McGinnis, *Parenting for Peace.*

CHAPTER 9 **responding to school commercialism**

1 Alex Molnar, "Cashing in on Kids: The Second Annual Report on Trends in Schoolhouse Commercialism" (Center for the Analysis of Commercialism in Education, 1999). Available at <www.uwm.edu/dept/cace/kidsreport/cashinonkids.html>.
2 Center for the Study of Commercialism, *Living in a Material World: Lessons on Commercialism, Consumption, and Environment,* (Tucson, Arizona: Center for Science in the Public Interest, 1996).
3 Walsh, *Selling Out.*
4 National PTA Guidelines for Corporate Involvement. Available at <www.pta.org/programs/guidelines1.htm>.
5 Recommendations available at <www.consunion.org/other/sellingkids/recommendations.htm>.

CHAPTER 11 **creating family traditions**

1 Ron Fox, "Supper at Home," in *Context*, #37, Winter 1994. Available at <www.context.org/ICLIB/IC37/Fox.htm>.
2 Wilkinson, *Caring for Creation.*

CHAPTER 12 **celebrating together**

1 Wilkinson, *Caring for Creation.*
2 Walsh, *Selling Out.*

APPENDIX I   **table graces**

come, Lord Jesus

Come, Lord Jesus, be our guest,
Let this food to us be blessed
By your hands must all be fed
Thank you God, for daily bread

Blessed be God who is our bread.
May all the world be clothed and fed.

heavenly father *(to the tune of Frère Jacques)*

(leader) Heavenly Father
(family) Heavenly Father
(leader) Once again
(family) Once again
(leader) Asking for your blessing
(family) Asking for your blessing
(leader) Amen
(family) Amen

back of the bread

Vs. 1: anon.
Vs. 2: Jeannie Trachsel

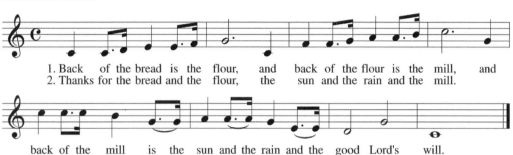

1. Back of the bread is the flour, and back of the flour is the mill, and
2. Thanks for the bread and the flour, the sun and the rain and the mill.

back of the mill is the sun and the rain and the good Lord's will.
Give us the strength from— day to— day to— do your will.

Used by permission.

come and dine

Words and music by
C. B. Widmeyer

"Come and dine," the Mas-ter calls us, "Come and dine. There is

plen-ty at God's ta-ble all the time." He who fed the mul-ti-tudes, turned the

wa-ter in-to wine, to the hun-gry now He calls us, "Come and dine!"

bapa terima kasih

Oh thank you, Fa - ther, thank you._____ Oh
Ba - pa t'ri - ma ka - sih,_____ Ba -

thank you, Fa - ther in heav - en._____ Oh
pa t'ri - ma_____ ka - sih,_____ Ba -

thank you, Fa - ther in heav - en. I thank you
pa di da - lam sor - ga, Ku ber - t'ri -

Fa - ther in heav - - - en.
ma_____ ka - sih._____

Used by permission.

come with hearts rejoicing

Words and music by
Lina Rauschenberg

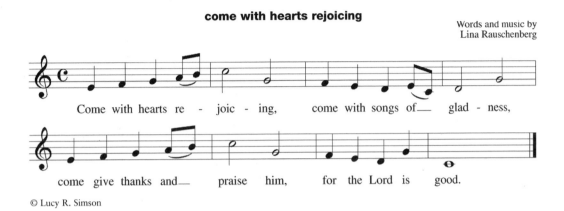

Come with hearts re - joic - ing, come with songs of__ glad - ness,

come give thanks and__ praise him, for the Lord is good.

© Lucy R. Simson

for the golden corn

E. Gould

E. Smith

For the gold-en corn and the ap-ples on the tree, for the gold-en but-ter and the

hon-ey for our tea, for fruits and nuts and ber-ries that grow be-side the way, for

birds and beasts and flow-ers, we thank you ev-ery day.

Harper Collins Publishers, London.

give to all creatures

Anon.
Trans. by Mary Ellen Meyer

Give to all crea - tures that live, their dai - ly por - tion. And feed our souls,

Lord, for they are yours and they live on your word. Make our hearts thank - ful for

your great good - ness. A - men.

thank you for the earth and sun

Daryl Nelson

Ted Lewis

Thank you for the earth and sun and for their fruits that make us one.

Thank you for each day we live and for— each chance— we have— to give.

Used by permission.

in the morning

Words and music by
Charles Neff

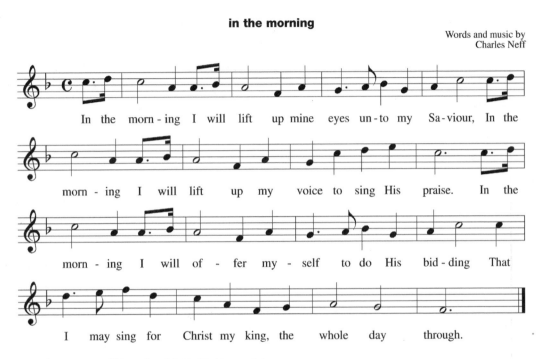

In the morn-ing I will lift up mine eyes un-to my Sa-viour, In the

morn-ing I will lift up my voice to sing His praise. In the

morn-ing I will of-fer my-self to do His bid-ding That

I may sing for Christ my king, the whole day through.

Copyright © 1944 Herald Press, Scottdale, Pa. Used by permission.

praise and thanksgiving
three-part round

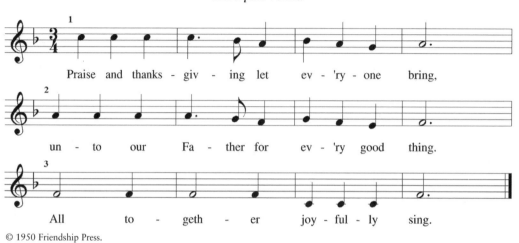

Praise and thanks - giv - ing let ev - 'ry - one bring,

un - to our Fa - ther for ev - 'ry good thing.

All to - geth - er joy - ful - ly sing.

© 1950 Friendship Press.

you, God, are my firmament

Words and music by
Miriam Therese Winter

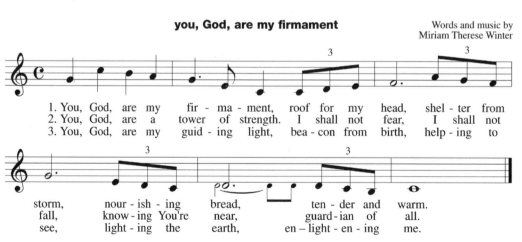

1. You, God, are my fir - ma - ment, roof for my head, shel - ter from
2. You, God, are a tower of strength. I shall not fear, I shall not
3. You, God, are my guid - ing light, bea - con from birth, help - ing to

storm, nour - ish - ing bread, ten - der and warm.
fall, know - ing You're near, guard - ian of all.
see, light - ing the earth, en - light - en - ing me.

Copyright © 1982, 1987 Medical Mission Sisters. Used by permission.

the morning song

Words and music by
Ted Lewis

We thank you, Lord, for the birth of this day out of dark-ness, out of the womb of night. Please help us now to prac-tice the way of the one who said, "Fol-low me."

Used by permission.

for health and strength

four-part round

For health and strength and dai-ly food we praise your name, O Lord.

Singing Every Day of Our Singing World, Boston, Ginn, 1950.

John Wiebe   **the servant's prayer**   Alan Dick
a call and response song

Cre - a - tor,   Re - deem - er,   Sus - tain - er,   New Birth,

thy will be done on plan - et Earth.   Heart of Sor - rows,

Ra - di - ant Sun,   Ho - ly   Pres - ence,   thy king - dom

come.   Hum - ble your peo - ple;   for - give our sin.

Heal our sick - ness;   cleanse with - in.

CHORUS

God   In - car - nate,   give re - lease;

on   paths of   jus - tice,   teach us peace.   In

*During the rests in each verse, the second singer or group repeats each phrase after it has been sung.

spite of in - dif - ference, ha - tred, and fear,

chan - nel our en - er - gies and keep us near. Show us the

truth, dear Moth - er of Love. We look with - in,

a - round, a - bove. Joy - ful

Fa - ther, hear our prayer; teach us to heal,

To Chorus

con - serve, and care.

Used by permission.

Thanks to the following for table grace contributions:

Anne Meyer Byler
Alan Dick
Peter and Elfrieda Dyck
Ted Lewis
Laura Lindell
Daryl Nelson
Dolores Siegenthaler
John C. Wiebe

APPENDIX II **resources for children**

BOOKS

children just like me   *Ages 9 to12*
Interviews and photographs from children around the world tell of their dreams,
beliefs, hopes, fears, and day-to-day lives. A sticker book and celebrations book
are also available. *By Susan Elizabeth Copsey, et al. Dorling Kindersley 1995.*

the biggest house in the world   *Ages 4 to 8*
A snail learns to create a huge masterpiece from his shell, only to find that he
cannot move it to search for more food. *By Leo Lionni. Alfred A. Knopf 1987.*

eco fun   *Ages 8 to 11*
Great projects, experiments, and games for a greener earth. Find out how to make
your own "green cleaners," become a kitchen sleuth, or create a forest ecosystem.
By David Suzuki and Kathy Vanderlinden. Douglas & McIntyre, Limited 2001.

the giving tree   *Ages 4 to 8*

Takes a poignant look at the art of giving through the relationship between a young boy and a tree. *By Shel Silverstein. HarperCollins 1986.*

the king's equal   *Ages 7 to 11*

An arrogant prince cannot become king until he finds a wife who is his equal. The clever Rosamund sends him to live in a hut in the woods where he learns humility, honesty, and hard work. *By Katherine Patterson. HarperCollins 1999.*

the quiltmaker's gift   *Ages 5 to 8*

When a generous quiltmaker finally agrees to make a quilt for a greedy king but only under certain conditions, she causes him to undergo a change of heart. *By Jeff Brumbeaur. Pfeifer-Hamilton Publishers 2000.*

rumpelstiltskin's daughter   *Ages 7 to 9*

Meredith and Rumpelstiltskin have a clever daughter named Hope who sells the golden coins spun by her father. The greedy king finds her and sets her to spinning gold in a cold palace cell. Hope cooks up a plan that results in prosperity for the people of the kingdom and her appointment as prime minister. *By Diane Stanley. William Morrow & Co., Inc. 1997.*

something from nothing   *Ages 4 to 8*

Joseph cannot bear to throw out his worn baby blanket that his grandfather made for him, so the grandfather always "fixes it" by using the fabric to make Joseph something "new." *By Phoebe Gilman. Scholastic Canada 1992.*

thank you, pooh!   *Ages 4 to 8*

Pooh Bear needs to get rid of ten old honey pots, so he gives them away to his friends who use them in creative ways. *By Ronne Randall. Golden Books 1997.*

tico and the golden wings   *Ages 5 to 8*

A beautiful bird travels the world giving away his golden feathers to those less fortunate. He learns a great lesson. *By Leo Lionni. Alfred A. Knopf 1975.*

the wump world   *Ages 6 to 8*

The "Pollutians" who take over the Wumps' beautiful world go on to decimate the landscape and pollute the air and water until even they can't stand it. Uncaring, they move to another planet. Meanwhile, the Wumps who fled the Pollutians to live underground, return to begin living above ground again. *By Bill Peet. Houghton Mifflin Company 1970.*

MAGAZINES (advertisement-free)

ladybug — *Ages 2 to 6*

spider — *Ages 6 to 9*

cricket — *Ages 9 to 14*

cicada — *Ages 14 and up*

Literary magazine for children with stories, poems, and art.
Carus Publishing Company, 315 Fifth Street, Peru, IL 61354.
<www.cricketmag.com>

national geographic world — *Ages 7 to 14*

Appreciation for creation and global connections.
National Geographic Society, Washington, DC 20036.
Phone 800-437-5521 <www.nationalgeographic.com>

potluck — *Ages 8 to 16*

Quarterly magazine of poetry, short stories, and book reviews by serious young writers. *Box 546, Deerfield, IL 60015-0546. <www.potluckmagazine.org>*

stone soup — *Ages 5 to 13*

Stories, artwork, and book reviews by young writers and artists.
Children's Art Foundation, 765 Cedar Street, Suite 201, Santa Cruz, CA 95060.
Phone 800-447-4569 <www.stonesoup.com>

story friends *Ages 4 to 9*

on the line *Ages 9 and up*

Monthly magazines of stories and activities that reinforce Christian values.
Faith and Life Resources, 616 Walnut Avenue, Scottdale, PA 15683-1999.
Phone 800-245-7894 <www.mph.org>

wild outdoor world *Ages 6 to 12*

Appreciation and understanding of wildlife and the outdoor world, use and
protection of natural resources.
Rocky Mountain Elk Foundation, PO Box 8249, Missoula, MT 59807-8249.
Phone 888-301-KIDS <www.wildoutdoorworld.org>

your big backyard *Ages 3 to 6*

ranger rick *Ages 7 to 12*

Animal stories and excellent nature photography.
National Wildlife Federation, Box 2038, Harlan, IA 51593.
Phone 800-611-1599 <www.nwf.org>

VIDEOS

child's view series   *Ages 8 to 13*

A set of short videos featuring children's daily lives in Bolivia, Cambodia, Congo, Haiti, Indonesia, Laos, Mozambique, Serbia, Thailand, and Uganda. *4 to 14 minutes each. Produced by Mennonite Central Committee 1991-2001.*

the lorax   *Ages 4 to 14*

A Dr. Seuss fable about how the destructive "Onceler" ignored the warnings of the Lorax and destroyed the truffula trees to manufacture "thneeds." When all the natural resources were used up, the Lorax gives this message: "Unless someone like you cares an awful lot, nothing is going to get better." *24 minutes. Produced by DePatie Freleng Productions 1972.*

the man who planted trees   *Ages 9 and up*

A lone shepherd restores a deserted hamlet ruined by loss of trees and drought singlehandedly planting a forest of thousands of oak trees over many years. Enables the viewer to see the impact of one person caring for the earth. *30 minutes. Produced by Canadian Broadcasting Corporation 1987.*

production notes   *Ages 10 and up*

Shows television commercials in slow motion while reading the production notes by the marketing agency. Demonstrates how ads target audiences and how TV commercials are constructions of reality. *28 minutes. Produced by Video Data Bank 1989.*

All videos are available for loan from MCC.
U.S. 888-563-4676   Canada 888-622-6337

rhythms of peace   *Ages 8 to 11*

Uses captivating stories and songs about peace and looks at the topics of prejudice, war toys, hate, and revenge. Includes conflict-solving ideas and a study guide. *56 minutes. Produced by Mennonite Media 1996.*

the rotten truth   *Ages 8 to 13*

Examines what happens to rubbish after it is thrown away. Encourages reduction of what we throw away by proving that you can't make nothing from something. *30 minutes. Produced by Children's Television Workshop 1990.*

where are the beans?   *Ages 11 and up*

Detective story examining the politics of food between North and Central America. *30 minutes. Produced by Mennonite Central Committee 1995.*

AUDIOCASSETTES

stories and songs of simple living   *All ages*

Popular storytellers and folk singers from various ethnic backgrounds share their works. *Available from Alternatives for Simple Living at <www.simpleliving.org>.*

we can solve it peacefully   *Ages 4 and up*

Explains and models negotiation in ways even preschoolers can clearly understand. The songs are catchy and clearly spell out steps to negotiation. The tape also includes dialogues modeling the process. *Available from Growing Communities for Peace at <www.peacemaker.org>.*

All videos are available for loan from MCC.
U.S. 888-563-4676   Canada 888-622-6337

WEBSITES FOR CHILDREN

WEBSITES

<www.kidsface.org> Kids for a Clean Environment is an international children's environmental organization.

<www.kidsplanet.org> A fun, interactive site by Defenders of Wildlife.

<www.nationalgeographic.com/kids> Includes games, discussion boards, activities, and contests for children.

<www.newdream.org/kids> Center for a New American Dream's kids site gives ideas for ways to play in noncommercial ways.

<www.nwf.org/kids> National Wildlife Federation's kids page includes several fun games, Ranger Rick's kids zone, and an environmental newsletter.

<www.ucsusa.org/game> The Great Green Web Game, by Union of Concerned Scientists, shows the environmental impact of consumer choices.

Note: This is a small sampling of interesting Websites for children. Parents may want to preview them first.

<www.youthactionnet.org> Seeks to connect, inspire, and nurture present and future young leaders by providing a virtual space where young people can share lessons, stories, information, and advice on how to lead effective change.

<www.zillionsedcenter.org> Information, polls, surveys, and fun—empowering kids to be savvy consumers and think for themselves. From *Zillions Magazine* and *Consumer Reports.*

APPENDIX III **resources for parents**

BOOKS

a call to peace: 52 reflections on the family pledge of nonviolence

Family devotionals focusing on relationships with people rather than things. *By James McGinnis. Liguori Publications 1998.*

caring for creation in your own backyard

Practical suggestions for families to serve as caretakers of a God-centered creation. *By Loren Wilkinson and Mary Ruth Wilkinson. Servant Publications 1992.*

a Christian view of money

Gives a theological basis for working with money and applies it to life situations. *By Mark Vincent. Herald Press 1997.*

the complete tightwad gazette

Fun-to-read suggestions on saving money and time. *By Amy Dacyczyn. Random House 1999.*

the consumer's guide to effective environmental choices
"Too many people drive their Land Rovers to the grocery store and think 'paper or plastic' is a meaningful choice." This book, from the Union of Concerned Scientists, helps sort out which lifestyle choices will have the greatest impact on the earth. *By Michael Brower and Warren Leon. Three Rivers Press 1999.*

extending the table: a world community cookbook
A thousand recipes and 300 stories from more than eighty countries around the world. Encourages people to learn from the world community. *By Joetta Handrich Schlabach. Herald Press 1991.*

feasting with God: adventures in table spirituality
Sixteen feasts and six culinary interludes to learn to respect food and feast in celebratory praise. *By Holly W. Whitcomb. United Church Press 1996.*

freedom of simplicity
Guide to learning to live in harmony with the rich complexity of life, and rediscovering simplicity. *By Richard Foster. Harper & Row 1998.*

how to teach peace to children
A practical guide for parents who want to make peacemaking a part of daily life as well as a global ideal. *By J. Lorne Peachey. Herald Press 1981.*

let's say grace: mealtime prayers for family occasions throughout the year
A collection of mealtime prayers to help families make prayer a meaningful and joyful part of everyday life. *By Robert M. Hamma. Ave Maria Press 1995.*

material world: a global family portrait

Families around the world emptied their houses of all their worldly goods for these snapshots. Beautiful and moving, it illustrates the reality of the three global classes. *By Peter Menzel. Random House 1995.*

our ecological footprint: reducing human impact on the earth

Explains how decisions about how to build houses, get to work, eat, and clothe ourselves affect the earth. *By William Rees and Mathis Wackernagel. New Society Publishers 1995.*

remember the time?: the power and promise of family storytelling

"The right story told at the right moment can turn a heart away from darkness, especially when the story makes the point." Chapters focus on various types of stories and conclude with questions and activities to generate storytelling in your family or group. *By Eileen Silva Kindig. InterVarsity Press 1997.*

a simple christmas: how to bring Christ and joy back into christmas

Offers hundreds of creative ways to keep the spiritual heart in the holidays and lead the family in doing things together. *By Alice Chapin. Herald Press 1998.*

simpler living, compassionate life: a Christian perspective

Essays and excerpts from Henri Nouwen, Richard Foster, Cecile Andrews, and nineteen other authors invite dialogue on time, money, food, spirituality, heritage, and community. *By Michael Schut, ed. Earth Ministry 1999.*

BOOKS FOR PARENTS

to celebrate: reshaping holidays and rites of passage

Encourages joy, spontaneity, justice, and concern for nature. An alternative to the models of celebration offered by a consumer society. Includes celebration experiences of people with widely varying backgrounds and perspectives. *By Eugenia Smith-Durland. Alternatives 1987.*

to dance with God: family ritual and community celebration

Examines each Christian celebration from a historical, psychological, and spiritual avenue. Ideas on how to incorporate celebration into the community, church, family, and self. *By Gertrud Mueller Nelson. Paulist Press 1987.*

unplug the Christmas machine

Suggestions to help focus your celebration on what is most meaningful to you. Ideas on how to reduce holiday stress through creating a spiritual celebration instead of a commercial holiday. *By Jo Robinson and Jean Coppock Staeheli. William Morrow & Co., Inc. 1982.*

your money or your life

Explores the difference between "making a living" and making a life. A process for keeping track of personal finances and weighing each expenditure by balancing how much of your life energy is spent with how much "life" it will bring. *By Joe Dominguez and Vicki Robin. Penguin Books USA 1999.*

VIDEOS

advertising and the end of the world

Extensively illustrated with graphics and examples from commercial imagery, this video presents a compelling and accessible argument about consumerism and its impact on earth's future. Challenges us to reevaluate our everyday practices and examine our commitment to future generations. *Produced by Sut Jhally 1998.*

affluenza and escape from affluenza

These videos explore the epidemic of shopping, overwork, stress, and debt that is infecting Americans in record numbers. Traces the historic roots, explores the marketing that sustains it, and offers concrete advice to find a cure. Shows people who work and shop less, spend more time with friends and family, volunteer in their communities and enjoy their lives more. *Produced by PBS 1997 and 1998.*

beyond the news: money

Examines money choices and encourages Christians to talk about the taboo topic of money and how being a follower of Jesus affects the choices we make. Includes study guide. *Produced by Mennonite Media 1995.*

beyond the news: TV violence and your child

Teaches how TV violence influences our behavior, emotions, and fears. Includes practical tips on how you can lessen the power of TV in your home. *Produced by Mennonite Media 1995.*

All videos are available for loan from MCC.
U.S. 888-563-4676   Canada 888-622-6337

break forth into joy: beyond a consumer lifestyle

Takes a look at lifestyle choices and the shape our lives have taken. Helps us realize how our obsession with buying and owning affects the earth, other people, and the human spirit. Calls us to a lifestyle that is more fulfilling and joyful. *Produced by Alternatives for Simple Living 1995.*

running out of time

Explores the social impact of time pressure and overwork on North American society, how much activity people fit into their busy lives, how much responsibility they increasingly assume, and how little leisure time remains. The program contrasts expectations about saving time with reality; compares conditions in other countries and at other times and examines solutions to overwork. *Produced by Films for the Humanities 1994.*

CURRICULUM

build a better world!

A four-session curriculum for vacation Bible school, camps and Sunday school settings. Features hope-filled stories of children assisted by Church World Service along with a related Bible study, poster, hands-on activities, and reproducible take-home sheets. *Available from CWS, PO Box 968, Elkhart, IN 46515. Phone 800-297-1516.*

All videos are available for loan from MCC.
U.S. 888-563-4676   Canada 888-622-6337

WEBSITES

<www.bozart.com>

Toys by artists that give your child the power of imagination.

<www.newdream.org>

The Center for a New American Dream is a nonprofit organization dedicated to helping individuals and institutions reduce and shift consumption to improve quality of life and protect the environment. Their motto is "More Fun, Less Stuff!"

<www.pbs.org/kcts/affluenza>

Explore the epidemic of shopping, overwork, stress, and debt in today's world with questionnaires, a time line, teacher's guide, links to other Websites, resources, and organizations with similar themes.

<www.simpleliving.org>

Alternatives for Simple Living is a nonprofit organization that equips people of faith to challenge consumerism, live justly, and celebrate responsibly. Includes an online catalog with books, videos, and cassettes on simplicity and parenting.

<www.tiddlywinktoys.com>

Quality unique and nonviolent educational toys reminiscent of the toys previous generations enjoyed.

CONTRIBUTORS

about the author: *Jeanne Zimmerly Jantzi* with her husband, Dan, and sons Benjamin, David, and Paul are currently serving with Mennonite Central Committee in Indonesia. They previously served in Congo and Nigeria. Jeanne enjoys travel, visiting, family fun, and lively philosophical discussions.

meditation contributors

Ann Weber Becker: Ann makes her home in Kitchener, Ontario, together with her husband, Byron, and their two boys Luke and Joel. Their church home is Manheim Mennonite Church.

Charmayne Denlinger Brubaker: Charmayne lives in Lancaster, Pennsylvania, on a farm with her husband, Omer, and sons Alex and Nick. She continues to value time and aims for a "handful with quiet rather than two handfuls with toil and 'chasing after wind.'" In her role as Human Resources director with Mennonite Central Committee this means working smart, being proactive, and planning ahead to minimize the inevitable surprises.

Rob Cahill: Rob and his wife, Tara, and their four children Nathan, Peter, John Paul, and Ruth are living and serving in Guatemala with Mennonite Central Committee. Together they enjoy reading children's books and spending time exploring God's creation with wide open eyes.

Rick Zerbe Cornelsen: Rick lives in Winnipeg, Manitoba, and is married to Dori, a pastor. He is particularly fond of his table saw and long summer evenings playing Stock Ticker in the screen porch with his children, Raya and Jonas. He also coordinates the Aboriginal Neighbours program of MCC Canada.

Angelika Dawson: Angelika lives and writes in Abbotsford, British Columbia, where she works in Communications for MCC B.C. and as provincial editor for *The Canadian Mennonite* magazine. She and her husband, John, have a 9-year-old son Aaron who is already rehearsing his acceptance speech for when he wins an Oscar for Best Director.

Eileen Klassen Hamm: Eileen knows how to make great compost, find lost mittens, create spaces for conversations and learning, and laugh. She works for MCC Saskatchewan focusing on gender and peace. Eileen lives in Saskatoon, Saskatchewan, along with her partner Les and their children Simon and Emily.

Marie Harnish: Marie lives in Indianapolis, Indiana, with her husband, Ned Geiser, and three children: Nathan, Hannah, and Luke. She is a mother, potter, organic gardner (organic landscaper), La Leache League leader, church and community volunteer, and enjoys reading.

Gerald Iversen: Gerald is National Coordinator of Alternatives for Simple Living in Sioux City, Iowa. He is an Associate in Ministry in the Evangelical Lutheran Church in America, a church musician, and a fundraiser/publicist for public radio. He and his wife Rita, a fourth-grade teacher, have two adult children.

Sue Klassen: After faith and her family, Sue's most important passions are for peace and justice, healthy child development, creating and maintaining hiking trails, and freelance writing. Sue is blessed to be able to pursue these interests while homeschooling her children Nathan and Sylvia with the support of her husband, Victor, and household member Kathleen Kern. She likes the values she sees their children choosing.

David and Heidi Regier Krieder: David and Heidi live in North Newton, Kansas. Heidi is a pastor at Bethel College Mennonite Church. She grew up overseas as the daughter of mission workers in Congo, and serves on the board of the new Mennonite Mission Network of Mennonite Church USA. David works part-time at Kauffman Museum, cares for their sons Benjamin and Mark, and is involved in a variety of wood-working and home repair projects.

Susan Mark Landis: Susan lives in Orrville, Ohio, with husband, Dennis, and children Laura and Joel. She is minister of peace and justice for the Mennonite Church USA. One of her greatest joys in life is when her children come find her, sit down, and talk nonstop about their day. It's double the pleasure when one of their friends joins in.

Mennonite Central Committee (MCC) is a relief, service, and peace agency of the North American Mennonite and Brethren in Christ churches. MCC has some 1,500 workers serving in fifty countries in food production, health, education, job creation, refugee assistance and peacemaking.

Mennonite Central Committee   <www.mcc.org>
21 South 12th St, PO Box 500, Akron, PA 17501-0500 USA; (717) 859-1151 or toll free (888) 563-4676
134 Plaza Drive, Winnipeg, MB R3T 5K9 CANADA; (204) 261-6381 or toll free (888) 622-6337